Confidence for Women

How to Be Yourself in a Way Where Self-Love, Self-Esteem, Assertiveness, and Happiness is Your Natural State, and Self-Doubt, Stress, and Anxiety is Not

© Copyright 2020

All Rights Reserved. No part of this book may be reproduced in any form without permission in writing from the author. Reviewers may quote brief passages in reviews.

Disclaimer: No part of this publication may be reproduced or transmitted in any form or by any means, mechanical or electronic, including photocopying or recording, or by any information storage and retrieval system, or transmitted by email without permission in writing from the publisher.

While all attempts have been made to verify the information provided in this publication, neither the author nor the publisher assumes any responsibility for errors, omissions or contrary interpretations of the subject matter herein.

This book is for entertainment purposes only. The views expressed are those of the author alone, and should not be taken as expert instruction or commands. The reader is responsible for his or her own actions.

Adherence to all applicable laws and regulations, including international, federal, state and local laws governing professional licensing, business practices, advertising and all other aspects of doing business in the US, Canada, UK or any other jurisdiction is the sole responsibility of the purchaser or reader.

Neither the author nor the publisher assumes any responsibility or liability whatsoever on the behalf of the purchaser or reader of these materials. Any perceived slight of any individual or organization is purely unintentional.

Contents

INTRODUCTION 1

CHAPTER ONE: WHAT IS CONFIDENCE? 3

    WHAT DOES CONFIDENCE MEAN? 3

    BENEFITS OF BEING CONFIDENT 5

CHAPTER TWO: COMMON CONFIDENCE ISSUES IN WOMEN 7

    DISAPPROVAL FROM AUTHORITY FIGURES 7

    TRAUMATIC CHILDHOOD 8

    DEALING WITH ABUSE 8

    PERCEPTIONS ABOUT APPEARANCE 9

    CAREER TROUBLES 9

    NEGATIVE WORK ENVIRONMENT 9

    SIGNS OF LOW SELF-CONFIDENCE 10

    INABILITY TO ACCEPT COMPLIMENTS 10

    SOCIAL WITHDRAWAL 10

    NEGLECTING SELF-CARE 10

    ANXIETY AND EMOTIONAL TURBULENCE 10

    OTHER PEOPLE'S OPINIONS 11

    SHY AWAY FROM CHALLENGES 11

Worried About the Future 11

Low Expectations 11

Inability to Trust your Judgment 12

Backing Away from Disagreements 12

Constantly Checking your Phone 12

Don't Speak Up 12

Everything is Personal 13

Blaming Others 13

Constant Explanations 13

Defensive Body Language 13

Making Excuses 14

Always Pessimistic 14

Need for Approval 14

Extremely Apologetic 14

Pointless Lies 15

No Boundaries 15

Inability to Enjoy Success 15

CHAPTER THREE: PERSONAL BELIEFS AND WHO YOU REALLY ARE 16

What Does a Belief Mean? 16

Are All Beliefs True? 18

Has a Specific Belief Worked Against You? 18

Figure Out the Source 19

An Alternate Meaning 19

Eliminating Negative Beliefs 20

CHAPTER FOUR: SELF-DOUBT- SILENCING YOUR INNER CRITIC..23

What is Self-Doubt? 23

Overcoming Self-Doubt 25

Being Real 25

STOP IT 26
STOP COMPARING 26
TALK TO SOMEONE 27
PEOPLE DON'T CARE 27
JOURNALIZING 27
NOT ALWAYS ABOUT YOU 28
SETBACKS ARE TEMPORARY 28
CHAPTER FIVE: 21 THINGS CONFIDENT WOMEN DON'T DO 29
CHAPTER SIX: 7 CONFIDENCE HACKS 36
HACK #1: ACT 'AS IF' 36
HACK #2: SPRUCE YOURSELF UP 41
Improving your appearance *41*
CHAPTER SEVEN: CONFIDENCE IN THE WORKPLACE 69
CHAPTER EIGHT: DATING CONFIDENCE HACKS 76
CHAPTER NINE: TAKING CARE OF YOURSELF 82
CHAPTER TEN: INFLUENTIAL WOMEN ON CONFIDENCE 89
CONCLUSION 92
RESOURCES 93

Introduction

Confidence might seem like an abstract concept, and there is no simple way to explain it. Some people might seem more confident than others, and you may wish to be more like them. Do you want to become more confident about yourself and the things you do? If yes, then this is the perfect book for you.

Most individuals tend to perceive confidence as believing in oneself, an idea, or someone else. Whenever a person displays confidence, they are, in fact, displaying their absolute faith in their talents, personal strengths, and abilities. When you feel confident, it tends to have a positive effect on your daily life, along with your ability to attain your goals. Confidence is directly associated with your self-esteem.

This book is the answer you have been looking for! In this book, you will learn about the meaning of confidence, general obstacles to confidence, understanding your personal beliefs, tackling self-doubt, and habits of a confident woman. Apart from this, you will also learn practical tips you can follow to improve your level of confidence.

Are you wondering, how is this book different from all the other self-help books present on the market today? For starters, all the advice given in this book is presented in an easy-to-understand manner. It contains proven methods and strategies along with expert advice you can use to improve your quality of life. As long as you are willing to make a conscious decision to follow the advice given in this book, you can see a positive change in your life.

These confidence tips are not just applicable to your personal life, but every aspect of your life. If you want to become more confident at your workplace, take control of yourself, and live the life you want, then look no further. This book has everything you need to become a truly confident woman. By following the simple yet practical advice given in this book, you can become more assertive, happy, and stress-free. This will allow you to get rid of any self-doubt and become a confident woman!

So, are you ready to learn more about all this? Are you ready to discover the secrets to becoming more confident? If yes, then what are you waiting for? Lets get started immediately!

Chapter One: What Is Confidence?

What Does Confidence Mean?

In simple terms, confidence is about having knowledge about your skills, abilities, and the value you provide. Not just this, it is also about behaving in a manner that conveys the same to others. Confidence differs greatly from low self-esteem or arrogance. Arrogance is the belief that you are better than others, whereas low self-esteem means you perceive yourself to be of less or no value. Confidence is personal, and it isn't the same for everyone. It tends to differ from one person to another. Different people have different levels of confidence. However, if you take a closer look, you will notice some signs that are common to all those who are confident, and it can give you a general idea of where their confidence comes from. If you're not a naturally confident person, then there is no harm in accepting this. There are ways in which you can build your level of confidence over time.

Do you ever wonder why some people are more confident than others? Confidence is a broad term. Defining it becomes a little tricky since it is so personal. Most individuals think of confidence as believing in oneself, an idea, or another person. Whenever someone displays confidence, they are displaying their faith in their talents, abilities, and personal strengths. When you feel confident, you have a positive attitude toward yourself and the world in general. No yardstick can be used to measure confidence. If you feel confident, then you probably are confident.

Self-confident people have certain qualities that others admire - it could be an orator who inspires others through his confidence and charisma or a doctor who is silently confident in his demeanor as he goes about his day. Self-confidence is extremely important in all aspects of your life. Low self-confidence is a common issue these days.

Self-confidence and success are closely related. Those who don't have self-confidence always find it difficult to achieve success. For instance, would you want to support a project pitched by an individual who keeps stumbling and fumbling for words? Well, you probably would not. On the other hand, had the same individual been loud, clear, confident, and had spoken assuredly and answered questions, the chances of considering his offer would have been high. A confident person can inspire confidence in others, and it is one reason why those with high levels of confidence are often successful in life.

If you worry that your self-confidence tends to waver, then stop worrying right now. Confidence is like a muscle; the more you train it, the stronger it gets. It is not a gift that people are born with, but it is a skill that is acquired. There are two ingredients to self-confidence, self-esteem, and self-efficacy.

Self-esteem is the way you cope with the happenings of your life and the acknowledgment of your inherent right to be happy. Your self-esteem might depend on the approval of others. However, most of your self-esteem stems from the fact that you have behaved virtuously and have the belief that you are competent at whatever you do. Whenever you work at improving yourself and achieve your goals, your self-esteem improves. It is the confidence you have in yourself that is required to be successful in life, and you need to be willing to make the effort required. It is a kind of confidence that prompts individuals to take up challenges and face life even when things don't seem to be going their way.

Benefits of Being Confident

Perhaps the two obvious benefits of being confident that you'll be more successful and happier in life. However, by digging a little deeper, you will realize there are more benefits you can enjoy by improving your levels of confidence. The more confident you are, the more you'll begin to value yourself and your abilities. It implies that you will feel more valuable and appreciated. When your level of self-esteem is high, you will be proud of yourself. You will naturally hold your head high and will not be worried about what others think.

For the reasons stated above, the more confident you are, the happier you will be with yourself. This makes it easier for you to enjoy the little joys of life without getting bogged down by worries.

When you doubt yourself constantly or question whether you can attain things in life, you are increasing your level of self-doubt. Self-doubt is the worst form of self-inflicted mental torture. If you are confident, then it becomes easier to avoid self-doubt.

The more confident you are, the better equipped you will be to deal with different situations in life. You will be able to learn, accept, handle, and even benefit from any circumstance you are faced with in life. Your mind will naturally tune itself to remove any fear and anxiety you might have previously encountered in a similar situation. When you are confident in yourself, you will be able to gauge any situation rationally without giving in to emotional responses.

When you start feeling more confident, you will feel more powerful and strong. You will become adept at tackling any problems that life throws at you. Whenever you are dealing with a testing circumstance, you will be able to face it bravely instead of feeling weak or defeated.

If you are secure about the way you perceive yourself, regardless of what others think of you, your social anxiety will reduce. You will no longer care about what others might think about the things you say or do. This, in turn, will make it easier for you to speak up and interact with others. Apart from this, you will also find the inner strength required to pitch your ideas and opinions without hesitation.

If you are confident and believe you can attain something, then you will naturally feel energized and motivated to work toward a goal. So, by improving your level of confidence, you can also improve your level of motivation to attain your goals.

As your confidence level increases, the amount of stress you experience will decrease. Apart from this, you will also feel like your life is comparatively less troublesome and free of unnecessary stress. So, if you want to be at peace with yourself and experience mental peace, developing your confidence is important.

When you are happy and confident, you will be more relaxed and comfortable - not just with yourself but with others around you as well. When this happens, conversations will flow more freely, and everything will be relaxing. So, your social interactions will not only become pleasant but even enjoyable. When you are at ease while talking with others, they will be more relaxed and at ease while talking to you.

When you are riddled with anxiety, fear, and stress all the time, you will not have any peace of mind. When you have peace of mind and are happier, then your ability to get a good night's rest will also improve. This will automatically improve your overall health. Confidence can make you healthy!

By now, you will have realized why confident people are more successful than those who have low levels of confidence. Now that you can clearly see the relationship between success and confidence, get to work immediately and develop those traits that will make you more confident.

Chapter Two: Common Confidence Issues in Women

Confidence is an important part of leading a happy life. Self-confidence enables you to believe in your abilities while maintaining a sense of competence in all aspects of your life. Low self-confidence tends to undermine your belief in your ability to stay competent and successful. Low confidence can also manifest itself in the form of inferiority, which can effectively prevent you from attaining any of your goals in life, or from growing. It is quite surprising that many people are not aware of their level of confidence or talents. Some might feel confident in one aspect of their lives and have extremely low self-confidence in some other aspect. Apart from this, many people also tend to have low self-confidence but are not aware of it, and this holds them back from attaining success in any form. In this section, lets analyze the most common causes of low self-confidence.

Disapproval from Authority Figures

A person's confidence can be severely impaired because of growing up with any disapproving authority figures. If you keep hearing that you are not good enough, you will believe that you are not good enough. This kind of negative self-image doesn't go away easily. We are all fond of approval. Approval is often the sign that others like what we are doing or saying. When a child is met with constant disapproval and harsh criticism, she will soon start believing that she has no redeeming qualities.

We all have an inner critic who keeps telling us we aren't good enough. With a little conscious effort, you can easily fix this negative self-talk. However, if your critic exists in your real-world and keeps telling you that you aren't good enough, you will eventually start believing this. If a child is met with harsh criticism, taunts, or disapproval, her self-confidence is bound to take a beating.

Traumatic Childhood

There are various reasons why your self-confidence isn't as high as it is for someone else. Childhood trauma is a common reason why children develop into nervous and anxiety-ridden adults. When not dealt with properly, it tends to have a lasting effect even in adulthood. Childhood determines and molds a person's life. Therefore, a turbulent or dysfunctional childhood can trigger feelings of inferiority and low self-esteem.

When a child doesn't get enough love and attention while growing up, she might start believing that she is not good enough and needs to change to get others to love her. Children from broken families or all those kids who grew up in households where there was constant fighting amongst the adults often blame themselves for everything that goes wrong. So, when the child grows up, she winds up being extremely apologetic, meek, timid, anxious, and riddled with inferiority.

Dealing with Abuse

Experiencing abuse in any form, whether it is physical, emotional, mental, or sexual can also lead to confidence issues. These kinds of traumatic events can make it quite difficult for a person to enjoy the world the way it is and trust themselves and other people. A combination of all these factors is quintessential to develop one's self-esteem. Even if one of these elements is missing, then personal self-confidence will be severely damaged. Abuse, coupled with trauma, can make any person feel emotionally empty. Apart from this, using any unhealthy strategies to cope with trauma can also harm one's self-confidence and self-perception.

Perceptions about Appearance

A common cause of low confidence is one's perception of appearance. All those people who find their appearance to be distasteful in some way or another struggle with confidence issues. A poor self-image is one of the main reasons they have low self-confidence. If they believe that others or society tends to look down upon their appearance for a specific reason, they usually shy away from social gatherings. Any perceptions about their flaws or even flawed perceptions about themselves are among the leading causes of a poor self-image. This self-image, when left unchecked, tends to have a severely negative effect on one's confidence.

Career Troubles

Perhaps you have a job that isn't in sync with the skills or abilities you possess. Maybe everyone at your place of work has more experience or is more qualified than you are. Maybe you have just joined a new place of work and don't think you can succeed. Perhaps you are overqualified for a job, and you feel it is beneath you. Being overqualified, underqualified, or having an inability to believe in oneself can all lead to a lack of self-confidence. You probably feel threatened by the way your co-workers behave or worry that you might end up losing your job. A combination of all these factors will certainly harm your self-confidence.

Negative Work Environment

If you have a bad relationship with superiors at your workplace, your self-confidence will take a beating. Apart from this, if you're surrounded by toxic co-workers, manipulative people, or anyone else who holds you back and doesn't allow you to excel, it will harm your self-confidence. Low confidence can also result from your inability to assert yourself. If others don't take you seriously or if others don't listen to your opinions, it has a cumulatively negative effect on your self-confidence. Since you spend a lot of your time at work, low self-confidence at work can easily trickle into other aspects of your life.

Signs of Low Self-Confidence

Perhaps you identify with one or more of the scenarios mentioned above. Are you worried that your low self-confidence might hinder your ability to grow in your personal and professional life? Well, before you can learn about developing your self-confidence, you need to understand the signs of low self-confidence.

Inability to Accept Compliments

How do you respond whenever someone compliments you? Do you say "Thank you" because you believe what they just said? Or do you try your best to deny the compliment or say something to downplay your achievements? Your inability to accept compliments is directly associated with your level of self-confidence.

Social Withdrawal

If you keep looking for excuses and reasons to get out of any social commitments or avoid making plans with people other than the ones who are absolutely necessary, it is a sign that you are low on confidence.

Neglecting Self-Care

If you don't take the time for self-care, it is also a sign of low self-confidence. If you think there is no point in taking care of your physical and mental wellbeing or don't pay attention to your physical appearance, it stems from a lack of self-confidence.

Anxiety and Emotional Turbulence

Whenever you are unsure of a situation or the potential outcome, it tends to cause anxiety. However, when you believe in yourself and have confidence in your skills, your anxiety and emotional turbulence will reduce. The lack of this self-belief is a cause for low self-confidence.

Other People's Opinions

Everyone is entitled to their opinion. If you keep worrying about what others think, you will not be able to live the life you want. If you spend a lot of time thinking about what others think or worry that others will not like you, it reflects poorly on your self-confidence. When you are confident, you will realize that your purpose of existence is not to make others happy. In fact, it is derived from living the kind of life that makes you happy.

Shy Away from Challenges

A confident person is not hesitant to take on any new challenges. In fact, they are proactive and will take on new responsibilities and challenges because they know it is desirable for their growth. If you avoid taking on any new responsibilities because you believe you will fail, it reflects your lack of self-confidence. You might probably believe that anything new is not worth your effort because you are already convinced that you will fail.

Worried About the Future

We all tend to worry about the future because we don't know what will happen. However, if you notice that you are always worried about the future, it might mean you have low self-confidence. This type of worry prevents you from enjoying your present and makes you extremely nervous whenever things don't come out as planned. A person with low self-confidence often believes that something or the other will go wrong and always waits for the ball to drop.

Low Expectations

Expectations might lead to disappointments, but not having any expectations is a sign of low self-confidence. If you believe that you will not be successful in life, or get much out of it, then you will stop trying. Accepting a mediocre way of life is not a positive sign. It almost seems like you have trained yourself to believe that some people are more successful because they are born with a special "something" that you lack.

Inability to Trust your Judgment

If you keep second-guessing yourself or are riddled with constant self-doubt, then it is because you don't have the confidence to trust your abilities. Maybe you don't believe you can make good decisions. If you constantly ask others for their opinions, it shows you are not secure with the decisions you make.

Backing Away from Disagreements

Disagreements are common. How do you react to any disagreements? Do you easily back out because you think you are wrong? In fact, you might even go to the extent of avoiding expressing your true feelings and opinions because of the fear of disagreement. Having a hard time speaking up or defending a specific view you share is a sign of low self-confidence.

Constantly Checking your Phone

You might keep relying on the phone as a means of getting out of any social situation. If you are at a social event or a social gathering, do you constantly check your phone? In fact, do you check your phone to the extent that you try to get away from conversations by doing this? If yes, then it is a sign of low self-confidence. You probably do this to feel like you're socially connected to make yourself look busy. The phone merely acts as a buffer, which prevents you from engaging in real conversations with others.

Don't Speak Up

If you keep second-guessing whatever you have to say or are plagued with self-doubt, then you will not be able to speak up during any group conversations. You might even hold yourself back, believing that whatever you say will sound silly. Since you're so afraid of what others will say or think, it becomes impossible to speak up. You might also believe that everyone in the group seems to be more knowledgeable than you feel and therefore hold your tongue. Apart from this, you might even wonder whether what you have to say is good enough to be shared.

Everything is Personal

A person with low self-confidence tends to take everything personally, especially criticism. Well, if you want to grow in life, you will need to deal with criticism. Your inability to stomach criticism or take it positively is a sign that you don't believe in yourself. If you react emotionally or become extremely defensive, it is a sign of low self-confidence.

Blaming Others

Constantly blaming others when things don't turn out like they were supposed to, is a sign of low self-confidence. The inability to shoulder any responsibility regardless of the outcome by shifting the blame onto others is a negative trait. Apart from this, if you notice that you constantly complain, then you might be suffering from low self-confidence. This is a common strategy where people assume the role of a victim who has little or no control over the happenings in their life.

Constant Explanations

Do you feel a constant need to keep explaining your actions, thoughts, or opinions? Everyone makes mistakes, but a person with low self-confidence often feels the need to justify their decisions, even if they are right.

Defensive Body Language

Using defensive body language, like stern facial expressions, or crossing your arms is a sign that you do not want to allow anyone else in and are trying to shut people out. By physically closing off your body language, it shows you are uncomfortable or anxious in the present circumstances.

Making Excuses

A person with low self-confidence often makes excuses to define their actions and choices, especially when criticized, so they don't seem inferior. To such people, accepting any form of personal responsibility feels like a sign of weakness. Well, accepting personal responsibility is a sign of inner strength and awareness. A person with low self-confidence fails to understand this. A confident person stops and listens to criticism without getting defensive. They can give a context to any criticism they receive.

Always Pessimistic

If you notice that you are always pessimistic or extremely critical of everything that happens, then it is a sign of low self-confidence. All the negative beliefs that are present within you tend to come out in the form of negative feelings. This kind of pessimism is the result of the feeling that you have no control over your own life.

Need for Approval

A confident person knows not to depend on external sources of approval to feel better. A person with low self-confidence, on the other hand, seeks constant validation and approval from others to feel better about herself. Not getting the approval that you need can also be a cause of frustration. A person with confidence issues is unable to understand the simple fact that not everyone will approve of her.

Extremely Apologetic

Apologizing shows you can understand when you make mistakes. However, constant apologies show that you don't trust yourself. Only apologize when you go wrong or hurt someone else. People with low self-confidence are incapable of understanding their true self-worth.

It prompts them to believe that everything they do is wrong, which makes them apologize.

Pointless Lies

A person with low self-confidence believes that the truth is not interesting. To make themselves seem more interesting, they tend to invent pointless white lies. If you don't feel like sharing the truth because you are worried about how others will perceive you, it is a sign of low self-confidence. If you tell white lies because you want others to think highly of you, it shows you don't love yourself.

No Boundaries

A person dealing with self-confidence issues might not be comfortable to draw and maintain personal boundaries. Establishing boundaries shows you love and care for yourself. Since you are worried about how others will perceive you, you always crave for the positive feedback. By establishing boundaries, you might not get this kind of feedback.

Inability to Enjoy Success

If you notice that you downplay your achievements or cannot enjoy your success, it is a sign of low self-confidence. If you associate your success with luck instead of the skills you possess, it is not a good sign.

Now that you have gone through the list of different kinds of low self-confidence, check off all those points you agree with. This simple exercise will help you gauge your level of self-confidence and make you aware of your behaviors, which will help you in your journey of building confidence.

Chapter Three: Personal Beliefs and Who You Really Are

What Does a Belief Mean?

A belief is a mental notion or assumption you have about yourself as well as the world in general. The thing with beliefs is that the mind tends to think these beliefs are absolute truths. Our beliefs can be tied to us emotionally and psychologically and are often irrational at the core. All the beliefs you have are a culmination of all the previous experiences and interactions you had with the world. This includes both good and bad experiences. Essentially, a belief defines your mental make-up.

Beliefs serve as a guide for our subconscious mind to function on autopilot. Once they are formed, they are deeply ingrained within us. We tend to take them for granted and believe them to be facts, regardless of whether they are true.

These beliefs firmly stick in our minds and can hinder our growth, especially when they are wrong. A negative belief can hold you back and does not allow you to capitalize on your full potential. Most of the beliefs you hold as an adult result from various childhood experiences. You might have picked up these beliefs from other people as well. For instance, whenever a child does something wrong, the parent might scold or criticize him for what the child did. As a result of this, the child might begin to believe that they are not good enough. This belief will influence any or all other existing and newly gained beliefs the child carries with him into adulthood.

There are two ways in which we form beliefs. Beliefs are either based on your experiences or inferences. Beliefs can also be based on things that others say, especially when you have accepted them to be the truth.

All the beliefs that are associated with relationships tend to be deeply rooted since these events are extremely emotional and have a lasting impact on one's subconscious mind. For instance, dealing with a nasty breakup might influence the way you perceive yourself. You might even start believing you are incapable of being loved or loving anyone else. Beliefs of this sort are negative and highly undesirable. Grab a sheet of paper and make a note of some beliefs you might have formed in your mind and have accepted to be the absolute truth.

You probably don't accept these beliefs on a conscious level but tend to react to them emotionally. Some instances of a few common and undesirable beliefs include the following:

- I am not good enough and will never be good enough.
- I haven't managed to achieve anything in life and will go nowhere.
- I am not smart enough, and that's why people don't take me seriously.
- I'm not capable of being loved, and I will never find true love.

Apart from these obvious beliefs, other common negative beliefs include thoughts such as, "I am too old, I am too young, I am not good looking, I am unlucky, I am useless," and so on. The list is endless. Start making a note of all the beliefs you have, and once you do this, you can become more aware of the beliefs that you hold.

Are All Beliefs True?

The next step is to understand whether your beliefs are true. Just because you believe in something doesn't mean that it is the absolute truth. Now that you're aware of all the negative beliefs you have in your mind, pick one of these beliefs and check whether or not it is the truth. For instance, if you think you are a bad writer, go down your memory lane and think of one article, letter, or anything you have written that others praised. If you believe that you are not good looking, then think of a time when someone complimented you. If you think you are not smart enough, then think of situations in your life you thought were impossible, yet you overcame them. This step is quite important because it allows you to understand that your beliefs are not necessarily true. You can go through your day thinking of all the things that contradict your beliefs. If you can contradict a specific belief, then let us move onto the next step.

Has a Specific Belief Worked Against You?

Think of all the different instances in your life where a specific belief worked against you. Perhaps it kept you away from doing something you always wanted to do or affected your overall personality negatively. It might have hurt your relationships, your state of mind, and even your general attitude or perception toward life. Think of all these instances and start writing them down. If you want to change something, then you need to take charge of the situation and do something about it. I believe pain to be an accelerant for change. When all your experiences have been a disappointment, then your willingness to change your life and shake things up a bit will increase. Now, you need to close your eyes and think back to all the painful moments and then visualize them. Make this visualization as real as possible and allow yourself to experience the pain all over again. You cannot change unless you really want to change. By visualizing these painful incidents, your willingness to change will increase.

Figure Out the Source

This step requires you to think a little deeper and go back to the memories of your past, preferably your childhood or teenage years. Now that you visualize an event that caused you pain, think about all the instances that led to this event. Think of the triggers and other factors that led to you feeling pain. Once you figure all this out, start writing them down and give yourself a detailed description of the event. When you close your eyes and start thinking about all the factors that led to a specific incident, it will even trigger emotions associated with a specific instance stored in your subconscious.

For instance, if you believe you are not good enough, then think of all the different reasons that led to this belief in your subconscious. It could be the comments made by others during your childhood. Another reason could be any disappointment expressed by authority figures in your life whenever you didn't behave in a manner that they expected. It could also be because of peer pressure you might have endured during early childhood and teenage years. Once you have identified the source, try to visualize that specific scenario and make it as detailed as possible.

An Alternate Meaning

The event you have identified in the previous step might not necessarily be the only reason for the negative beliefs you have formed. In fact, it might not even be fully true. Just because someone in your high school thought the essay you had written wasn't good enough doesn't mean you are a bad writer. You might have believed a specific belief because you thought it was the irrefutable truth. In reality, it just means you adopted a specific perspective that was negative and went ahead with it. You didn't even test any other alternative yet plausible explanations for a specific situation your belief stems from.

A particular situation can have different meanings apart from the one that you have attached to it. The event influences you because you allowed it to influence you. Now, think of all the reasonable alternatives you can think of for a specific situation. You might be able to come up with alternate meanings when you think about it from the perspective of a neutral party. Go back to the instance when you thought you were a bad writer; there was likely some other plausible explanation. Perhaps the teacher was having a bad day, or maybe your style of writing differed from that which the teacher expected. Perhaps it was just nervousness.

Similarly, if you think you're not good enough, then think of the alternate reasons why your parents might have reacted harshly. Perhaps they were upset about something else, and when they said you are not good enough, it was just a single moment of anger. Now, try to visualize this same situation, but allow your newly gained alternate explanations to influence the way you feel about it. Once you do this, you will realize that you have the power to lend meaning to any situation. If you think you are not good enough, then it is because you have allowed yourself to believe you're not good enough.

Eliminating Negative Beliefs

Here are three simple steps you can practice in order to remove many negative beliefs from your mind.

The first step is to close your eyes and visualize a scenario that has contributed toward forming the negative beliefs. Now, imagine that this scene is slowly fading away until it becomes hazy and distant. It almost feels like someone has turned out the lights, and you are still trying to see. Now, visualize the scene slowly moving away. As the scene starts pulling away from your mind, allow it to become blurry. Keep doing this until it becomes nothing more than a distant memory and it shrinks into nothingness. You will be left with darkness. Now, breathe in slowly and breathe out slowly. Take a couple of deep breaths and allow your mind to calm down.

In the second step, slowly open your eyes and write down a statement that contradicts a specific belief you have. For instance, if you believe you are a bad writer, or you are not good enough, make a note that you are a good writer and you are a very warm and loving person. This step requires you to write something that isn't consistent with the beliefs you already have in your mind.

The third step is to remove the negative beliefs from your visualization. Close your eyes. Try to visualize how you would feel if the statement you had written in the previous step was true. Visualize that you are a good writer and are working on a book on your laptop in an elegantly furnished office. Perhaps you can visualize yourself walking in a lush green meadow on a sunny morning, knowing fully that you are a wonderful person. Think about all the different details in this scene. What are the different things that you can see in this visualization? Are there any specific sights or smells you can experience? Are there things in your visualization that you can touch? Think about all these things and allow yourself to feel every emotion with no judgment. Once you do this, you might end up smiling. Now, try to make your visualization a little brighter as if someone has turned the spotlight on your visualization. When you go through all the steps, evaluate how you feel and think if the situation still bothers you.

Your actions and beliefs are closely related. If the way you act is not in sync with your beliefs, then those beliefs will slowly fade away and lose their credibility. It essentially paves the way for a new set of beliefs that are validated by signals generated by your new behaviors. It might sound a little complicated, but it is quite simple. It all boils down to the way you talk to yourself and think. If you start talking and behaving like a confident person, your confidence levels will increase. When you start feeling confident, your perception changes, and from this perception, new beliefs are formed. Motivation is also closely associated with confidence. Therefore, the more confident you are, the more motivated you will be in life.

Most of us tend to forget that we are the creators of our own beliefs and that we are the only ones who have the power to change our beliefs. Keep in mind that there is more to a situation than the way you interpret it. Just because you think something is true doesn't necessarily mean it is true. You have the power to change your perspective, and only when you change your perspective will you be able to change your beliefs.

If you are keen on changing your limiting beliefs, then start using the different tips given in this chapter. All that you need to do is carefully read through the steps discussed, grab a paper and pen, find a quiet spot for yourself, and start writing your thoughts. It will give you a better understanding of your beliefs and how to change them.

Chapter Four: Self-Doubt- Silencing Your Inner Critic

What is Self-Doubt?

Experiencing self-doubt is all too common, and most of us will have experienced it at one point or another. However, what matters is the way you deal with it, how you cope with it, and what you do with it. It makes all the difference between chronically struggling with self-doubt and allowing it to pass you by. If you keep regularly experiencing self-doubt, you might ask yourself, why does everyone else seem to do well when I'm struggling?

To a certain extent, self-doubt is healthy. Self-doubt enables you to understand when you're not doing something right. With self-doubt, you tend to question and challenge yourself, which prompts internal inquiry. Self-doubt can also bring about humility and increase your understanding of others.

The society we live in values the extraordinary. Therefore, it is common for self-doubt to become a chronic state instead of a fleeting one. When it becomes chronic, you often stand in your own way, and it leads to self-sabotaging thoughts. Even when things are going well for you, you might struggle to see the good. This kind of self-doubt is unhealthy. When you cannot see your good qualities, it becomes difficult to stay motivated. You might believe you will never attain your goals, don't have the talent required, or are unworthy of any position you hold. Any small failure you encounter becomes proof of your perceived sense of unworthiness. Unhealthy self-doubt is like a parasite that consumes you from within while reducing your self-worth, self-esteem, and self-efficacy.

There are certain psychological mechanisms used by self-doubt to perpetuate their unhealthy attitudes toward themselves. For instance, if you're worried that you will not pass an exam, you might be tempted not to study at all. By doing this, you can easily associate the blame of your failure to not studying or the lack of preparation. It is quite an innovative way to shift all the blame away from ourselves and onto an external factor. You can reassure yourself by saying that it was not you who failed, but the situation itself that led to your failure. Had you studied harder, you might have passed. Since you didn't study, you did not pass. This kind of belief is self-sabotaging. Since it stems from the fear of failure, you will always be scared. It is also a reason people tend to procrastinate. If you keep at it for too long, you will eventually reach a situation where you believe you cannot succeed because regardless of what you do, failure is the only potential destination.

The way you talk to yourself repeatedly forms certain dents in your neural pathways. If you keep telling yourself you are incapable of doing something or you are not good enough, these thoughts will become a part of your psyche, and you will believe them to be the truth. This self-fulfilling prophecy is based on the notion that "I cannot." When you convince yourself that you cannot do something, the effort you make will also reduce. If you are going to fail, then what is the point in trying? With less effort, you tend to increase your chances of failing, which in turn reinforces your negative beliefs and ends up creating a rather vicious cycle.

If you don't celebrate your achievements, it is because of a lack of self-kindness. You might be supportive and nurturing towards all those you love, yet you may be critical of yourself. The absence or lack of self-kindness leads to self-doubt. When you are kinder to yourself, it becomes easier to embrace your deficiencies and improve yourself. All those individuals who have a higher level of self-doubt often seek approval from others. They tend to worry more about their failures and negatively evaluate all the situations, which leads to unnecessary self-judgment. It also increases the risk of isolation.

Another factor that is associated with self-doubt is impostor syndrome. It describes an unreasonable feeling of being an impostor where, in fact, all the achievements you attained are accredited to luck instead of your personal abilities and effort. You probably believe that it is only a matter of time before others discover that you are a fraud in disguise. Anxiety and depression are commonly accompanied by impostor syndrome. By giving credit to all your achievements to external factors instead of your own self, you prevent yourself from successfully seeing your self-worth.

Overcoming Self-Doubt

William Shakespeare once said that our doubts are traitors, and they make us lose out on all the good in life because we fear failure. Self-doubt not only holds you back from acting on opportunities, but it also makes it difficult to start and finish things. The good news is, you can easily overcome self-doubt, provided you make an effort to create change. Self-doubt stems from the internal negative self-talk and wrong beliefs you have formed about yourself. Here are different steps you can use to overcome self-doubt.

Being Real

It is time to be real with yourself. Ask yourself this simple question, "How many times when I feared the worst did it actually become a reality?" Well, if you are honest, then it might not have happened as often as you thought it would. Self-doubts are like the imaginary monsters that kids fear before going to sleep at night. They tend to prevent you from making any changes and keep you well within your comfort zone. If you want to develop and excel in life, you need to step outside your comfort zone.

Take some time and carefully analyze your past. Think about all the instances where things progressed smoothly despite your doubts. Once you realize that not all your self-doubts are based on facts, it becomes easier to let go.

Stop It

Whenever you feel that your internal self-talk becomes negative, tell yourself to stop. You can control your thoughts. Instead of allowing them to spin out of control, you can quickly discourage them. If you feel yourself questioning your own motives, try to talk to the doubtful part in your psyche. You can easily disrupt any patterns of negative self-talk by telling yourself to stop. You can scream at your internal critic to quit being negative. Don't allow your thoughts to control you. Instead, learn to control your thoughts.

Stop Comparing

If you keep comparing yourself to others or to the successes they have attained, it becomes easier to doubt yourself. Since we live in a world where we are surrounded with constant social media posts about others living the perfect life, it becomes tempting to compare oneself with these projections. Instead of comparing yourself to others, compare yourself to yourself. When you spend some time and analyze your life, you will see all the progress you have made. You are your worst enemy and your best competition. The only person you need to outdo is yourself. Think about all the obstacles you have overcome in your life and all the negative circumstances you have successfully navigated. There might have been some instances in your past where you thought it was the end of the world. Well, it wasn't, and the proof is the fact that you are here today! Congratulate yourself on making it this far and keep pushing forward.

Talk to Someone

When you keep all your thoughts to yourself, they often become distorted and exaggerated. It might also reach a situation where they are no longer reasonable. All this is true with self-doubt. To remove yourself from such a situation, it is always a good idea to talk to someone else about it. Once you let go and say these things out loud, you will hear how exaggerated your self-doubt has become. When you talk to someone you trust and love, you might be able to see things from a different perspective.

People Don't Care

A person with extremely high levels of self-doubt often believes that others think about what they say or do. When you start worrying too much about what others think or say, self-doubt tends to get a stronger hold over you. Whenever this happens, remind yourself that people don't really care that much. After all, everyone has their own lives to deal with. Even if they make any negative remarks, it all stops there. Things will not bother you unless you permit them to do so. People have to think about themselves, their jobs, or any other aspect of their lives. Since they have all this to do, they won't have that much time to worry about you. So, forget about what others think. It is not your job to change the way others perceive you. As long as you are true to yourself, you have nothing to worry about.

Journalizing

Maintaining a journal is a very good idea in terms of dealing with self-doubt. Maintain a realistic account of your life. Don't forget to include the positive aspects of your life while writing the negative ones. After all, life isn't always that bad. If you look for it, you will realize that there are many things to appreciate in your life. When you start writing down your doubts and fears, it becomes easier to gain a sense of clarity. All the things you are worried about might not seem that catastrophic once you write them down. Apart from this, it also gives you a better perspective of the issue at hand.

Whenever you are facing a challenge, start writing the list of pros and cons of different solutions you can use. This is a rational and logical way to deal with a challenge instead of worrying about failure.

Not Always About You

Regardless of what you might choose to believe, everything isn't always about you. Whenever someone criticizes you, it is easy to start doubting yourself. When someone rejects you on a date, it is difficult not to take it personally. However, what if the things others said were never about you? Perhaps your boss criticized you because he was having a bad day at home. The guy you were on a date with didn't want to go on another date because he was still hung up on his ex. Perhaps he had other commitments to deal with. When you think about all the incidents in your life from the perspective of someone else, you will realize that the world doesn't revolve around you. Instead of readily accepting blame for everything, analyze the situation from the other person's perspective.

Setbacks are Temporary

Nothing in life is permanent. Even if it feels like you're going through an incredibly tough time right now, it will pass. A setback is a temporary situation, and you have the power to overcome it. Keep in mind that you are not a failure because you failed in a specific situation. The true failure is when you refuse to learn from your experiences. Everything that happens in your life happens for a reason. Once you understand the reason, you will be a better version of yourself.

Start following these simple, practical tips, and you will see a change in your internal attitude toward yourself and life.

Chapter Five: 21 Things Confident Women DON'T Do

When you think of some confident women like Oprah Winfrey, Malala Yousafzai, Meghan Markle, or even Hillary Clinton, what do these ladies have in common that makes them so fearless in life? They all carry themselves with an air of unapologetic grace, success, and unfettered determination. The energy changes whenever they enter the room. In this section, let us look at a couple of mistakes you must avoid if you wish to become a confident woman and how you measure up in terms of self-confidence.

1. Don't Give in to Self-Doubt

Self-doubt is common, but a confident woman knows not to pay attention to unnecessary self-doubt. Hesitation is not a natural part of how they process things, and they seldom second-guess their own decisions. They often know what they are doing and the reasons for doing them. They spend the time required to think about their decisions thoroughly, and once they have decided, nothing can stop them.

2. Don't Worry About Trends

A confident woman is not someone who follows trends but is a trendsetter. Don't waste your time thinking about what is "in" or what society thinks you should to do. Instead, all the choices you make must be based on your personal preferences. Confident women are well aware of their needs and preferences. They don't hesitate to ask for what they want, because they believe they deserve everything that they want.

3. Don't Waste Time Gossiping

Nothing wastes time quite like gossip. Confident women don't talk about other women and don't waste their time gossiping. Instead, they focus all their time and energy on talking about their goals, dreams, plans, and aspirations.

4. Not All Opinions Matter

Everyone has an opinion, but a confident woman understands not to base her decisions on what others think or feel. She might listen to others, but every decision she makes is based on her own conclusions. She will never listen to any advice blindly, rather, she will do her own fact-finding to understand what she must or must not do.

5. Don't Suppress Your Feelings

Confident women don't attempt to suppress their feelings. If there's something on their minds, rest easy knowing that you will know it. They are not worried about calling things as they see it. With confidence comes the ability to speak one's mind freely and openly in a way that others will listen to.

6. Don't Worry About Pleasing Others

Confident women are not people pleasers. If they want to do something, they will do it. They are self-assured, and their self-confidence is not based on external sources of approval. They are true to themselves and fully trust their intuition. A confident woman not only has the ability to hear her heart but also has the strength to handle any opposition. Since she doesn't waste all her time trying to make others happy, she is a happier person.

7. Don't Ignore Self-Care

A confident woman knows that she is responsible for her wellbeing. She would never compromise on self-care. She understands the importance of maintaining a balance between her personal and professional life. She takes the time required to eat healthy meals, sleep properly, and even spend time pampering herself. She does all this because she knows it is in her best interest.

8. Don't Have Any Regrets

Confident women not only learn their lessons from their past experiences, but also understand all the mistakes and poor choices they might have made. They do this having no regrets. The ability to learn from the past and improve oneself is a sign of self-confidence. Instead of wasting their time worrying about all the things they could have done differently, they know what they are supposed to do.

9. Don't Confuse Failure with Defeat

Confident women don't think of failure as the ultimate defeat. They know that every failure they come across is merely a stepping-stone to success. They are the ones who will tell you the number of times Henry Ford went bankrupt before he became extremely successful. They understand that the path to success is never smooth, and there are plenty of bumps along the way. They experience failure like everyone else, but they also know how to learn from their mistakes and keep moving forward.

10. It is Okay to Get Messy

A confident woman knows that it is okay to get messy. Even if they value making good first impressions and like to look good, they don't care if they get their hands dirty to attain their goals. They will not be bothered if they are caught in a rainstorm or get dirt on their hands while tending to their needs. They know how to look at the positive in every situation regardless of whether they are stuck in a horrible downpour or experience a nasty fall.

11. Don't Forget your Purpose

Confident women understand their purpose in life and use this to guide all the decisions they make. They are not the ones who would go about their day like a headless chicken. Instead, these determined women know precisely what they want and how they can attain their goals. Once they have a goal in mind, nothing can stop them. They don't make any unconscious decisions, and every risk taken is calculated. This fearless way in which they live their lives is what makes them extremely magnetic to others.

12. Don't Worry about Peer Pressure

Giving in to peer pressure is something many people do, especially the ones who don't have their own opinions or beliefs. These people always give in to what others want them to do. Since confident women understand what they want without trying to please others, it is easier for them to avoid the stress of peer pressure. Peer pressure is reserved for people who worry too much about what others think. A confident woman doesn't have the time to indulge in this unnecessary worry.

13. Always Be Productive

Productivity is often confused with being busy. You can be busy doing a hundred different things, but it doesn't mean you are productive. Productivity is making the most of the time and resources available to you in order to attain any objectives you set for yourself. A confident woman knows not to glorify this aspect of being busy. Confident women are productive and always concentrate on getting the job done. Since they are getting things done, they don't feel overwhelmed by all the tasks they have to accomplish.

14. Don't Ignore Your Instincts

Even if everyone thinks one thing, or facts point to something different, confident women will always go with their intuition. They know that they are not supposed to ignore what their instincts are telling them. Intuition is the little voice in your head that tells you that something may be amiss. If something doesn't feel right and your gut says so, then pay heed to it. When it comes to decision-making, gut instinct is your biggest ally. Confident women not only understand this but aren't scared to trust their gut. Your intuition or gut instinct is based on a millennium of evolution and tries to protect you in any dangerous situation. Ignoring your gut instinct is not something you should do.

15. Silence isn't Uncomfortable

Silence doesn't have to be uncomfortable, and a confident woman knows this. She knows how to be content even when there is no one around. Her source of comfort is internalized and not based on any external sources. She has the awareness to accept herself and her thoughts. Therefore, silence seldom bothers her. Silence only bothers those who cannot deal with their thoughts. If you make peace with your thoughts, you will feel comfortable too.

16. Don't Take Everything Personally

Confident women know not to take others' opinions personally. They know that everyone is entitled to their opinions and that the opinion of others doesn't reflect poorly on them. They might value the input from others but will not be too bothered if such opinions don't support their personal beliefs. If you take everything that everyone says personally, then you will merely make yourself unhappy. In the end, the only person who will feel bad is you.

17. Don't Fret Over Materialistic Possessions

A confident woman knows better than to equate who she is as a person with what she has. Confident women don't allow materialistic possessions to define who they are. They may or may not live in the swankiest houses or use the latest gadgets because they know their self-worth. Instead of allowing petty possessions to define them, they define themselves. They live their lives based on what they want and not live how others think they should.

18. Quality and not Quantity

Confident women know the value of authenticity. In fact, they will value it more than being popular. Instead of having hundreds of friends and millions of followers on social media, they value authentic relationships they share with a select few. Quality always comes before quantity for confident women. They love challenging conversations and don't aspire to be popular because they know it doesn't matter in the end.

19. Don't Need External Motivation

Confident women don't need others to support or believe in them. They have the internal motivation and the desire to succeed. They know what needs to be done. They are their personal cheerleaders. They don't need personal trainers or alarm clocks to motivate them to do things they need to do. Their internal motivation drives them to get a jump on the day without hitting any snooze buttons. The kind of clarity they have about their desires and wants gives them the motivation and the courage to work toward achieving them.

20. Don't Deny Yourself

A confident woman knows not to deny herself. She understands that there needs to be balance in every aspect of life. Apart from this, she also knows that every function has a limit. She will never try to stretch herself thin or push herself to her breaking point unnecessarily. She will try to improve herself continuously but will not take on any unnecessary stress. She knows that to be truly happy, she must not deny herself. So, even if she is on a diet, she will not feel guilty for occasionally treating herself to ice cream. She might love going to the gym regularly, but she knows the world will not end if she doesn't exercise for a day. She knows what she wants and will unapologetically work towards attaining those goals.

21. **Don't Chase Perfection**

Not everything in your life will go exactly in the manner that you have planned. There will be setbacks. Things happen. We might mess things up. Obsessing too much over things and making your happiness dependent on outcomes will do you no good whatsoever. You will need to learn to be happy despite your circumstance. We tend to get in our own way. We do this without realizing it. You will need to quit worrying about a specific outcome. Things will happen, and there will be things that are beyond your control. The only thing you can control is your actions. You cannot control the situations you are in. You should stop worrying about getting a specific result. Instead, concentrate on how you can make most of what's given to you. If you try too hard to get a certain result, you will get in your own way. Desperation will not get you the results you want. It will just hinder your growth. Stop trying to fit in where you don't belong. If the shoe doesn't fit, it is time to move on. Find something that you are comfortable in.

Confident women know that others don't have to like them. Perhaps this is one of the main reasons why everyone seems to like them and aspire to be them. Now that you've gone through the list of things that confident women ***don't do***, it will become easier to gauge yourself. If you notice that you do certain things that these women don't do, then take action today to change yourself.

Chapter Six: 7 Confidence Hacks

Did you ever notice that some people seem more confident than others? It might also feel like confidence is an inherent trait that only a select few have been blessed with. Well, this isn't true. Confidence is a skill much like any other. So, even if you lack self-confidence, you can easily work on improving yourself. It takes time, commitment, patience, and plenty of conscious effort to develop this trait. However, once you get the hang of it, your confidence levels will soar! In this chapter, let us look at practical tips you can follow to improve your levels of confidence.

Hack #1: Act 'As If'

Did you ever come across the phrase "Smell your fear"? Well, fictional characters and people in the real-life often talk about animals and humans smell fear on others. It can conjure up images of a snarling dog or a knife-wielding psychopath. Yes, humans can smell fear. Human communication doesn't take place just via spoken word, but also visual means. Friends, loved ones, customers, potential business partners, and other prospects can smell your fear.

You probably think you're putting on a good facade to come across as being confident while engaging in conversation with others, or even while making a presentation. However, if you don't feel genuinely confident about yourself, then people can see through your facade, and they can see your lack of confidence. It can be extremely harmful to your ability to succeed because people will not believe you if you don't believe in yourself. Confidence is a very contagious emotion. If you don't feel confident about yourself, you cannot expect others to feel confident about you. For instance, no one will want to engage in a business prospect with you if you don't feel confident about yourself and the business that you are trying to start.

We all face circumstances where we doubt ourselves. Even the most confident people experience self-doubt from time to time. It is natural to doubt yourself, especially when you find yourself in an unfamiliar situation or around strangers.

Confidence is like a big balloon that can either soar high in the sky or deflate depending on how you feel about yourself. Your confidence can take a backseat, especially if the criticism comes from someone you love or respect. For instance, a child in school can feel absolutely crushed if her favorite music teacher tells her that she cannot play the lead in a musical because of her weight or her body type. Even if the child was never conscious of such a thing until the incident, she would certainly become conscious of herself later.

Keep in mind that your parents cannot revive your confidence for you, and even your friends cannot. They can certainly make you feel better, but confidence needs to come from within. You cannot expect others to make you feel confident. Likewise, if your confidence stems from external sources, then it can get shattered easily. Confidence is a state of mind. Much like happiness, the key to feeling more confident is in your hands. If you are willing to work on yourself, you can become as confident as you want.

If you have a goal, don't quit, as you need to keep going. Whenever you take on something new, doubt and fear start cropping up in your mind. It is a signal that you're supposed to take stock of your inventory of skills and knowledge to ensure that you can succeed. Whenever these feelings signal that you are missing something important, pay attention to them. Missing an important piece of information or skills can lead to a potential disaster. For instance, you can electrocute yourself trying to rewire the house if you don't know what you're supposed to be doing.

At times, these feelings and signals can be misleading. Fear and doubt crop up while you are learning something new or are trying to grow in life. These kinds of experiences are quintessential for success, like when you take on a project you have never attempted before or are trying to learn something new for the first time.

So, how can you develop confidence in situations like these? How can you show that you are confident when you don't feel confident? The only way to feel more confident is by overcoming your fear and self-doubt. Two important factors create self-confidence. The first factor is to believe in the project, as it should be in line with your dreams. The second factor is to believe that you have what it takes to attain your objectives. The first factor is relatively easy to deal with when compared to the second one. If someone somewhere else at some point has done something you are trying to attain, then your goal is achievable. Now, this brings us to the second part of the equation, which is relatively tricky, because when you have the required skill, knowledge, and abilities, you might not have enough confidence in yourself. If you want to be successful in life, then you need to understand there is always a certain risk involved in everything that you do. You cannot grow or attain your goals in life if you don't take on risks. Even if you believe you can succeed, there will be risks involved. So, make your peace with this and take the first step. However, don't take any foolish risks, always take calculated risks.

The simplest way to begin feeling more confident is to use the 'act as if' technique. This technique mainly uses your natural mental and emotional responses to bring about thoughts and behavior that will make you feel more confident. When you don't feel confident about something or yourself, your mind concludes that despite the circumstances, you are a beyond your abilities or understanding. The physical response of your body to these thoughts is to become tense, and your mind responds to it by digging up memories along with thoughts that reaffirm the fears and doubts you have.

Your emotions might further the perception that the circumstances you are in are bigger than you can handle, and it restarts the cycle once again. It is a cycle of natural response that connects your basic thoughts and actions. The 'act as if' technique helps reverse this reaction cycle by changing the way you think and the way you act. If you want to increase your confidence, then you need to behave like you are confident. So, let us start with your posture. When you are running low on confidence, your body mirrors your state of mind, and you tend to shrink or slouch unknowingly. Instead, make a conscious effort to sit with your back straight and keep your shoulders held high. Lift your chin and always look straight ahead instead of slouching.

Next, concentrate on your breathing. Taking in shallow and rapid breaths is a sign of hyperventilation and nervousness. Once you start breathing calmly and deeply through your nose and slowly exhale, your body will start to relax. After changing your posture and the way you breathe, you will be more relaxed. Continue this process by opting for clothes that reflect what you are trying to attain. Start behaving, thinking, and talking as if you have already attained the goal you want.

For inspiration, you can always look at those who have achieved the goals you want. Pay attention to the way they behave, walk, and talk. If you're not able to understand what you're supposed to do, then you can copy them. Imitate the way they talk and walk. It doesn't mean that you have to mimic every single aspect of the personality, just copy those things that spell confidence. The final step to this exercise is to think about yourself differently. It is time to shush your inner critic and change the way you talk to yourself. Instead of wasting your time thinking about all those memories that reinforce your self-doubt and fear, think about all the circumstances in your past when you overcame challenges and attained your goals.

Here's a simple affirmation you can use whenever you feel a little low on confidence. "This is a new challenge I am facing, but I have overcome difficult obstacles in the past." Reinforce your self-confidence by telling yourself that you have all the skills and knowledge you require to get the job done. Even if you don't have the skills right now, tell yourself you can always learn about them as you progress.

Once you start behaving as if you have attained your goals, your emotions will start to settle, you will be able to relax, and you can think about all the challenges that lie ahead of you. When your mind starts believing that every circumstance you are in is perfectly manageable, it becomes easier to feel more confident. Concentrate on consciously encouraging your mind to reinforce positive thoughts and emotions. Armed with the feelings of confidence and boldness, you will soon be able to take the necessary steps required to attain your goal, and within no time, you no longer have to 'act.'

This technique doesn't work if you are trying to pretend to be confident. People can see right through any facade that you put up. This technique works because it instils confidence in yourself by changing your perception or perspective of the situation you are in. If you think something is unattainable, then attaining it will become difficult because you believe it to be impossible. It essentially helps reprogram your mind and the nervous system to respond favorably toward any challenges without creating any dents in your self-confidence. This technique is not the only way in which you can become more confident. However, it is one of the simplest ways in which you can become more confident, and it is easy to follow.

So, whenever you are running low on confidence, remind yourself that you are a confident woman who can achieve whatever she puts her mind to. Consciously correct your posture, breathing, and your actions. By following these three simple steps, you will start to feel more confident and in control of your life.

The 'act as if' technique can not only be used to improve your level of self-confidence, but it works very well for other emotions as well. If you want to be happy, then start acting happy. Think happy thoughts and behave in ways that happy people usually do. Always keep a smile on your face, hold your head high, enjoy yourself, play, and have some fun. If you do all these things, eventually, you will feel happier. This technique is based on the law of attraction. The law merely states that you receive what you give out to the universe. So, if you send positive vibes out into the universe, the universe sends positive vibes back to you.

Hack #2: Spruce Yourself Up

You've probably heard the saying that beauty is just skin deep. Well, inner beauty matters more than outer beauty, but looks do matter. When you look good, you tend to feel better about yourself. Various factors directly influence your self-esteem, and physical appearance is one of them. Any perceived flaws you have about your looks could be a source of distress. In extreme cases, it can lead to mental disorders like social anxiety, eating disorders, or even body Dysmorphic disorder. In simple terms, low self-confidence about your looks can adversely affect your overall mood. So, let us look at simple ways in which you can spruce yourself up to improve your level of self-confidence.

Improving your appearance

The first step is to figure out the triggers that affect your confidence. Do you feel more confident when you dress a certain way? Do you feel less confident when you don't spend enough time to groom yourself? Is your confidence dependent upon the group you spend more time with? Are there any other issues like your relationship status, or your employment status that trigger low self-confidence? Your self-perception sometimes triggers low self-confidence.

The second step is to concentrate on the way you perceive your physical appearance. Think about your source of self-esteem, question any negative beliefs you have about your looks, and think of ways in which you can change your beliefs about your physical appearance. While analyzing all these things, start writing down your observations.

Make a note of three things that you like most about your physical appearance, and three things about your personality that you like the most. It could be something as simple as volunteering at a local charity or maybe even calling your friends right away when they need someone to talk to. If you don't appreciate yourself, you cannot expect others to appreciate you. You need to love and respect yourself unconditionally if you want to change the way you think about yourself.

Humans are vain, but not a lot of people accept this. It is perhaps one reason why most of us talk about having a wonderful personality more than looks. It is okay to concentrate on personality traits, but it is not okay to forget about physical appearance.

Now, it is time to make a list of your three best personality features. Maybe you love your curly hair, your limbs, or even your smile. Make a list of your three physical features that you love the most. It is time for a little self-introspection. Stand in front of a full-length mirror and think about all the different thoughts that come into your mind the minute you see your reflection. Are all these thoughts based on your self-perception, or are they based on the opinion of others? Try to understand the accuracy of the opinions that have been made about you. Are you taller than others? Are your hips wider than others? Are you too skinny? Do any of these things matter?

If one of your friends came to you because she was having a body image crisis, how would you talk to her? Would you try to reassure her or criticize her? If you are compassionate toward others, then it is time to extend the same compassion toward yourself. Concentrate on replacing all negative thoughts with positive ones. Instead of concentrating on your perceived negative attributes, concentrate on the positive ones.

We are constantly bombarded by different images or notions of the perfect and ideal body on social media. Keep in mind that just because someone perceives something to be the perfect body type, it doesn't mean you need to live up to the same perception. Most of the images of celebrities you see these days have been thoroughly airbrushed and photoshopped. Don't try to live up to an unrealistic perception of beauty. Work on reframing positive thoughts about your body. For instance, if you think that your nose is too big or your eyes are too small, remind yourself that these features make you unique.

Make a habit of writing at least three positive things you love about yourself. Before going to sleep every night, record these thoughts in a journal, and keep doing this daily. It will be a positive journal. So, whenever you start feeling low on self-confidence, you can quickly go through your journal and feel better about yourself.

Changing your style

Researchers at the Harvard Medical School in the USA conducted a study, along with the University at Chieti in Italy, to test the influence make-up can have on women. One hundred and eighty-six women took part in this study, and it was conducted to determine whether the "lipstick effect" is a true phenomenon or not. The lipstick effect is used to describe a psychological phenomenon where a woman feels more confident and attractive when she wears make-up. Well, the study showed that women feel more confident after wearing make-up that suits them. So, it is safe to say that your level of self-confidence also depends upon how you feel about yourself. By merely changing your style, you can feel more confident.

Start wearing clothes that make you feel comfortable. You don't have to compromise on style for the sake of comfort or compromise on comfort for the sake of style. Start by recognizing your unique sense of style and dress accordingly. Certain trends and styles might look good on celebrities and models but might not necessarily suit you. So, learn to recognize what does and doesn't suit you and dress accordingly. You don't have to follow the latest trends to look good blindly.

The clothes you wear must highlight the physical features you favor. Always dress according to your body shape and learn how to flatter your body shape. There are different basic body shapes and understanding the various types of clothes that accentuate your best features means you can dress in a way that suits you. For instance, avoid wearing dark colors and monochrome if you are skinny. If you have broad shoulders and long limbs, then wear clothes that concentrate on your limbs! It is simple, but it takes a little preparation.

Start wearing well-tailored clothes or the ones that fit you well. Even a gorgeous woman can look like a sack of potatoes if she wears ill-fitting clothes. If you find no clothes that fit you well, then you can always get them tailored.

Wearing the right shade of lipstick and applying the right kinds of make-up can make you feel better about yourself. Choose the right color of lipstick based on your lip color. For instance, bright shades of red and pink-colored lipsticks look good on women who have pale lips, and warmer shades look good on the ones who have dark lips. While applying make-up, ensure that you are using make-up based on your face shape. For instance, if you have a rather rounded face, then use make-up to define your cheeks and eyes instead of concentrating on your lips. There are different tricks you can use to uplift your natural features instantly. In fact, there are plenty of YouTube tutorials and videos you can use for inspiration.

Get a good haircut that matches your face shape and highlights your natural beauty. Just because bangs look chic on your favorite actress doesn't mean they will suit you. If you have a square face or a strong jawline, then getting layers to frame your face will help soften the sharp facial lines you have.

Spend some time and concentrate on keeping yourself well-groomed. Create a daily, weekly, and monthly grooming routine for yourself. Ensure that you always keep your nails clean and well-trimmed. You don't necessarily have to get a manicure every ten days, but it is entirely up to you. Brush your teeth at least twice a day to improve your oral health and hygiene. Always carry wet wipes with you to freshen up, even while traveling. Drink plenty of water to keep your skin thoroughly hydrated. Apart from this, invest in the right beauty products like concealer, bronzer, an eye shadow palette, lipstick, and so on based on your skin tone. Start washing, moisturizing, and cleansing your face before going to bed at night. Using a good fragrance can also instantly change the way you feel about yourself.

Experiment with different styles until you find one that works well for you. It is a process of trial and error, so be a little patient.

Regardless of who you are, or the state of life you are in, you always have the power to make yourself feel better. Don't give up on yourself and don't fall into a cycle of self-loathing. If you want to feel your best, then you need to look your best. When you feel positive about yourself, then the way you look at life will also change. There is nothing frivolous about beauty. It is quite empowering and can positively influence your state of mind. Feeling good about yourself is powerful. There is a direct relationship that exists between your inner and the outer beauty-the way you think about yourself is the way others think about you. Beauty can be used to bring about a positive change in your life and start using it today.

Your self-confidence is greatly influenced by the way you perceive yourself and your physical appearance. By following these simple steps, you can improve your physical appearance. Not just your physical appearance, it also creates a positive change in the way you perceive yourself. Once you are happy and satisfied with the way you look, you will feel more confident. Apart from this, simple tips will also ensure that you are taking good care of yourself. Self-care is also important for self-confidence.

Hack #3: Think Like a Goddess

You might have come across different quotes on the Internet, or social media like "You are a goddess, just remind yourself of it." These quotes are supposed to be motivating and inspirational. However, the message that they send seems to be along the lines of, "You are flawless, and you don't have to work on yourself." Well, this isn't true. We all have flaws and accepting them is important. There is always a scope for improvement. Believing oneself to be flawless differs from loving oneself despite the flaws.

Hearing that you are amazing or awesome doesn't cause any changes within us, even when we know it isn't the truth. As soon as you hear the truth, you might not want to hear it. Being criticized by others or our inner critics is seldom pleasant. Well, nobody is perfect, and you don't have to be perfect. Don't try to be.

By allocating a self-care day, taking a bubble bath, or spending hours together at the spa might make you feel better. However, all this is just fleeting, and self-care is so much more than this. Self-care is about an attitude and mindset instead of a bubble bath and pedicures. Taking care of your physical, mental, and emotional wellbeing must be your priority. Look at your reflection in the mirror and tell yourself certain positive attributes about your body. Self-care is not a destination, and it is an ongoing journey. If you want to feel confident about yourself, or anything you have achieved, then it takes time, effort, and patience. To feel confident, you will need to work on yourself. By meditating for an hour or spending the day at the spa, you cannot feel confident. It must be an ongoing thing.

Everyone keeps talking about accepting one as a goddess. What does the Goddess mindset even mean? The truth is, it isn't the lack of capability, skills, experience that tends to hold most of us back from attaining our goals. It is about having the right emotional mindset.

This mindset is known as the Goddess mindset. It is based on the simple belief that you need to believe you are worth it. It needs to be one of your core beliefs. A Goddess mindset is about creating a positive belief in yourself and tapping into your internal goddess. It is about learning to harness the energy that is present within yourself to improve your confidence. It is about loving yourself unconditionally and cherishing your body, mind, and soul.

Unless you truly embody the goddess that you are, you cannot unlock your actual potential. There is so much more to you than the mere tags the society uses to describe you. You could be someone's daughter, mother, wife, sister, granddaughter, friend, confidant, and so on. Well, you are more than these tags describe. You need to understand that you are all this and much more. The way you feel about yourself determines the kind of energy and people you attract into your life. Once you learn to awaken and embrace your inner goddess, you will feel unstoppable.

There are many different things that can destroy your self-confidence. It could be because of any family issues, turbulence in your professional life, or the simple perception that you are not enough. Someone could probably look at you in a way that makes you uncomfortable. Various people in the form of bullies, unfaithful lovers, abusive co-workers, or troublesome bosses can bring you down. Situations can also bring you down, such as not getting the job you wanted, dealing with a divorce or a breakup, or being ghosted by a person that you thought you connected with. Pretty much anything under the sun can affect your level of confidence. When all these things develop over the years, confidence tends to take a backseat. It distracts you from connecting with your natural goddess.

Regardless of whether you find your soulmate, the perfect house, the perfect job, or even live the perfect life, learning to accept your inner goddess is important. Reconnecting with your inner goddess and finally understanding the goddess mindset will help you regain your confidence. Allow no one to tell you that you don't deserve to live the kind of life you want. If you truly want something, then the entire universe will help make it come true.

Here are the simple steps you can use to reconnect with your inner goddess.

Start believing in yourself. See yourself for who you truly are and work on improving yourself every day. Try to be the best version of yourself and always put your best foot forward. It doesn't mean you need to hide your insecurities or your flaws. In fact, it means the exact opposite of it. It means you need to embrace yourself, and every aspect of your being. If you don't like something about yourself, you can always work on changing it. A goddess is someone who doesn't doubt herself, her capabilities, or her beauty.

Don't hide your flaws or ignore them. Learn to accept your flaws and love them because they make you who you are. Your flaws make you unique. Don't try to chase the mirage of perfection. Instead, be the kind of person you want to be. Do these things for yourself and not because of what others say or think.

Start wearing clothes that make you feel confident and sexy. Don't worry about what society will think or say. People will talk regardless of what you do. Instead of holding yourself back, unleash your inner goddess.

The environment you surround yourself with reflects your beliefs. You probably have certain dreams based on the good feeling you think will be yours one day when you attain your dreams, right? The trick to manifest that good feeling associated with the dream into reality is by feeling good at this moment. You don't have to wait for an uncertain future to feel good; you can start feeling good this instant. This good feeling will help you attract good into your life.

Do your surroundings at work and home reflect your sense of style and make you feel good right now? If they don't, then it is time to work on improving your environment immediately. You can start by decluttering so that your space is dedicated to only those things that add value to your life and help achieve your dreams. It is about allowing the free flow of energy around you. When you are surrounded by an environment conducive to good vibes, you will automatically feel good.

Add all those things that inspire and motivate you and eliminate everything else. Don't clutter yourself with unnecessary things. Decluttering is a great way to prioritize your needs and wants. When your surroundings are well organized, it brings about a sense of order and clarity. These positive aspects will have a positive effect on the way you think. For instance, a cluttered desk might stifle your creativity. So, unclutter to unleash your inner goddess.

You need to talk like a goddess as well. It is not just the way you talk to others; your self-talk matters. Most of us are good at criticizing, comparing, and judging ourselves. All this kind of negative dialogue tends to cause more harm than good. It is okay to take some time for self-introspection and understand the different aspects of your life you would like to change. However, indulging in excessive self-criticism will harm your self-esteem and self-confidence. Negative self-talk leads to unnecessary damage of any issue you are dealing with. This kind of criticism can also prevent you from thinking rationally and clearly. If you're in a critic keeps telling you that you are not good enough or that you are not enough, you will soon start believing that as well. Get rid of all disempowering thoughts and beliefs. To do this, you need to pay attention to what you think and your internal self-talk. Once you start regulating it and replace all negative beliefs with positive ones, it is empowering.

Whenever you notice any self-sabotaging thoughts pop into your head, try to change it. Initially, it takes plenty of conscious effort, but after a while, it will come to you naturally. For instance, what is your first reaction whenever you are faced with an obstacle? Do you believe that the obstacles are the end of the road or that you will not be able to overcome them? Well, this is just negative thinking at play. Instead, think of it as an opportunity to learn and grow. Maybe there is a chance that has been presented to you in life to improve yourself. Keep in mind that everything that happens in life happens for a reason. If you look hard enough, then you will realize that every cloud has a silver lining. It is merely about the way you view and perceive things.

Another great way to bring about positivity into your life is via positive affirmations. Start using daily affirmations to reaffirm your self-confidence. The simple daily affirmations you can use are as follows:

- I am a confident woman.
- I am brilliant.
- I accept and embrace my flaws because they make me who I am.
- I am an incredibly sexy woman.
- I love the person I am.
- I am grateful for every experience I have had, both good and bad, because they define me.

Money is certainly an important aspect of life. Ignoring it or believing that it is unnecessary is rather naïve. However, it is important to understand that money is not everything. That being said, it is an important factor that contributes to the way you feel about yourself and the confidence you have in yourself. How do you feel about prosperity and your finances? Are you one knowingly sabotaging the flow of money into your life because you don't see it in your bank balance right now? This tends to happen whenever you unintentionally dishonor whatever you have right now by believing that what you have is not sufficient.

If you believe that you have no money, or that you will never have enough finances, then you are not attracting positivity into your life. Therefore, it is time to replace all this with a little positivity. Dealing with your finances is an overwhelming task, and it is difficult. The simplest way to go about doing this is by keeping track of every single penny that comes your way. Even if a penny doesn't seem like much right now, but they all add up, and eventually it fattens up your bank balance.

Learn to understand your worth and work on improving yourself. Always keep a positive attitude in life and don't let any negativity bring you down. Every negative encounter or experience you have in life is a learning lesson. Don't allow it to extinguish the power of your inner goddess. Embrace the goddess mindset, and you will see a positive change in your overall life and attitude toward life.

Hack #4: Crack a Smile

You might have heard the lyrics of an old song that goes something like, "When you are smiling, the whole world smiles with you." Well, it turns out this song is right, and smiles are quite contagious. Yes, you read it right - smiles are contagious. When you see someone smile at you, don't you smile at them automatically? It is a knee-jerk reaction that takes even if you don't know the other person.

We all have different subconscious needs, and perhaps the deepest emotional need of all is the need for self-esteem. A vital means via which the subconscious need for self-esteem can be fulfilled is through acceptance. Who would not want to be liked and accepted just the way they are without changing anything? One of the major reasons for lack of self-esteem and self-confidence these days is the lack of acceptance or rejection from certain groups are individuals and society. If you keep expressing your unconditional acceptance of every person you meet - not just at home, but even at work - you will soon be amongst the most popular people across the world. How can you express your unconditional acceptance? Well, start smiling.

It only takes 12 facial muscles to smile, whereas it takes 113 facial muscles to frown. Whenever you genuinely smile at someone, it conveys a positive message that the said person is pleasant, likable, or even attractive. A single smile is so powerful that it can quickly uplift someone else's low self-esteem. Not just that, when you smile, you are sending positive vibes across to someone. It kicks starts the reaction when that person sends positive vibes your way. And the cycle keeps going on.

Make a conscious habit of smiling as much and as often as you can. While smiling, ensure that your smiles are genuine and not faked or forced. People can see through a fake smile. It doesn't take much to smile, and it is quite a simple thing to do. If you are unable to smile, then think about a couple of positive thoughts and experiences you had in your life, or even the people who make you laugh, and a smile will automatically appear on your lips.

Whenever you smile at anyone else, it kickstarts a physical reaction where endorphins are released in your body. Endorphins are feel-good hormones that instantly elevate your mood. These endorphins not only make you feel happy, but they also improve your self-esteem. When you smile, you start thinking and even start acting in a way that is more personable to all those around you and give out positive energy. A common behavior that a lot of popular and influential people share is that they always have a genuine smile pasted on their face. Whenever you smile, you are not only making others feel good, but you are also actively improving your self-esteem. This is also an important factor that determines your ability to have healthy and lasting relationships in your life. You cannot have a healthy relationship with someone if you don't smile. It all starts with a smile, and there is no end to the different benefits you stand to gain.

All it takes is one deliberate decision to smile at the people around you and to express that you are genuinely happy to have met or seen them. Being negative will certainly not make you popular. In fact, people will not be comfortable approaching you if you don't smile or have a glum look on your face all the time. The thing with human beings is that we all tend to take everything personally. Even if you look cranky or grumpy for no reason, others might think that someone has done something to upset you. So, to avoid all these unnecessary misunderstandings, it is better just to smile.

Whenever you find yourself a little low on energy or need a little extra motivation, try smiling. Take a couple of minutes out of your routine and think about all the things in your life you are truly grateful for. It could include worldly possessions and all the people you cherish and value. Once you start counting your blessings and express your gratitude, a smile is bound to show up on your lips.

Several researchers have long compiled the list of benefits associated with smiling. It is believed that smiling can make you look a lot younger than you are. Even if there is no other benefit from smiling, this might prompt a lot of people to try to smile more often. Whenever you smile, others tend to perceive you as being a little younger than you are. When you smile, it adds a sparkle to your eye, and this is probably the reason why you look a lot younger. Also, smiling is like giving your face a mini facelift. It turns up the corners of your mouth and raises your entire face including your neck, jowls, and your cheeks. Instead of wasting precious money on getting cosmetic procedures and facelift, it is better to opt for a natural solution that is smiling. If you don't want to look like you are burdened by the troubles of the entire world, then smile and do it often.

When the corners of the mouth are turned down into a frown, it probably gives the impression that you are weighed down by plenty of unhappiness. Why give off a negative impression to someone else? Everyone has their own problems, and everyone is dealing with them. The easiest solution to this problem is to smile.

It is believed that smiling can improve your overall sense of wellbeing while elevating your mood. As mentioned earlier, smiling releases endorphins in your brain. Apart from this, serotonin and dopamine also releases into your system. These hormones directly influence your mood and uplift the way you feel. Endorphins share similar properties with opiates, and they are your body's natural defense against pain. So, the phrase, "smile through your pain," is quite true. You can reduce your body's perception of pain when your nervous system is overrun with feel-good hormones.

The kind of pleasure that smiling induces in your brain is quite similar to the one you feel whenever you eat chocolate. So, you can be quite happy without consuming any extra calories and improve your mood. You no longer have to depend on food to make you happy. All that you need to do is smile a little more. Smiling is simple, and it helps you feel better about yourself.

Even if it is not a natural smile, even for a smile can act as a mood boost. Whenever you think about the positive experiences you have had in life or any happy memories, you tend to smile. By merely deciding to smile, you tend to give your mind a positive experience to concentrate on. The source of your joy doesn't have to be anything else other than your smile. So, if you feel a little blue, smile and instantly uplift your mood. You might have heard others tell you to put on a happy face. Turns out, putting on a happy face actually makes you feel happier.

Apart from all this, smiling tends to make you seem more likable, courteous, and competent. If you seem scared, worried, sad, or anxious, then others might wonder what is troubling you. If you want to seem more confident, then start smiling. It is a simple psychological trick that makes others trust you. For instance, if you have a major presentation that you are worried about, don't frown. By smiling, you are immediately sending a message across to the audience that you know what you are doing and that you are confident about yourself. Fake it 'til you make it, right?

Smiling will not only make you feel better about yourself, but it can make others feel better about themselves, too. If you notice that one of your coworkers is having a hard day at work, why don't you smile at him? You don't have to do anything else, just try sending a few positive vibes to him.

Now that you understand the direct relationship between smiling and your self-confidence, it is time to smile more often. However, there are some things you must consciously try to avoid. You can fake a smile or two, but don't mask all your emotions by smiling. Always analyze your emotions before you decide what to do about them. It is never okay to ignore or forget about any emotions you feel. If you don't deal with your emotions constructively, they all tend to bubble up to the surface and come out negatively. To avoid any unnecessary emotional outburst, try to understand what you are feeling and the reasons for the same. Once you have carefully analyzed all this, then you can decide whether or not you want to smile.

If someone smiles at you, can you discern between a fake and a genuine smile? If you can do this, then others can do it too. There is a distinct difference between a genuine and a fake smile. If your smiles are genuine, you will feel better about yourself, but it will also make you seem more genuine and personable to another person. If you don't want to come across as being fake, then try to control the fake smiles you display.

A smirk differs greatly from a smile. Be aware of how your face looks when you smile. If you keep smirking, you'll come across as being unapproachable. This is not what you're trying to do, is it? If you have heard someone say wipe that smile off your face, then maybe you should look at the way your face looks when you smile. Work on projecting a smile that says you are happy - and also confident.

In certain situations, smiling can seem a little submissive. Just because you are smiling, doesn't mean you need to agree with what others have to say. Even if something displeases you, you can convey your displeasure while smiling. You don't have to try and please everyone else, but there is a way in which you can let others down gently.

Hack #5: Use Power Poses

The idea of power poses has been steadily gaining popularity in recent years. Unless you have been completely off-grid, you will have heard this phrase. Power poses are body postures that are designed to make you feel more confident and powerful. By assuming certain postures, you can signal your mind that you feel confident, in control, and ready to face any challenge that comes your way.

Perhaps the most popular poses of all are the wonder woman poses. It is a strong body position where you stand with your feet apart, head lifted high and your back straight, and your hands placed on your hips. You might wonder whether these positions work, and if so, how they work.

Amy Cuddy has been accredited with the popularization of power posing. Power posing can greatly influence your state of mind as well as your behavior. By assuming certain strong and confident poses, it tends to cause changes in hormone levels by increasing the production of testosterone while reducing cortisol, a stress-inducing hormone. Testosterone is believed to be a hormone that makes one biologically dominant, confident, assertive, and more relaxed because of the reduction in stress-causing hormones.

When you start behaving more confident by assuming these positions, you tend to feel more confident as well. By placing your body into positions which are normally associated with the idea of power and dominance, you feel all those feelings you desire. By following power posing, you are essentially faking it until you become what you desire.\Power posing certainly affects the way you feel naturally about yourself and the way you protect yourself from the rest of the world. By improving these two things, you will feel more confident about yourself and the choices that you make. Power posing affects the way others perceive you as well. Since these positions are often associated with power, control, strength, and confidence, others will also perceive you as being powerful, confident, in control, and strong. Body language and body positioning is an important aspect of non-verbal behaviors. Most of the communication that takes place is not just through words spoken by verbal communication, but it is to non-verbal communication. Body language is what non-verbal communication is all about.

Power positioning merely refers to making certain nudges or tweaks to your regular body language to make yourself feel more confident. Power posing also makes others perceive you as being more confident. Whenever you are plagued by self-doubt or worry, try power posing to dispel all these unnecessary fears and worries. Power posing creates a mind-body nudge that helps shift the flow of your emotions in a desirable direction. It allows you to avoid any psychological stumbling blocks that can halt your progress and slowly destroy your self-confidence. Even if you don't feel all-powerful and confident, power poses will help change all this. However, it doesn't happen immediately. You need to keep practicing it daily and consistently to see positive and lasting changes.

A simple pose you can practice within the comfort of your own home is the victory pose. If you have ever watched a sporting event that you love, you may have noticed the joy with which the winners jump around to celebrate their victory. Whenever an athlete wins the race, scores a goal, or experiences any other form of victory, the common physical reaction is to raise their arms high above their heads with a closed fist to celebrate their win. Well, you are essentially required to imitate these actions to make yourself feel triumphant and victorious. You don't have to use this pose when you win, but you can start reverse engineering. Start with the feeling of triumph and the feeling of happiness and slowly make your way back to the task at hand. If your mind is already thinking like a winner, then you will automatically feel more confident about whatever you are pursuing.

Now, let us move onto the simple salutation pose. In this pose, you are required to plant your feet firmly on the ground, lift your head and chest, and outstretch both of your arms upward toward the sun. It is almost like you're standing on the ground attempting to reach out to the sun with your arms stretched wide in an inviting hug. This is a power pole; you must start practicing daily to feel more confident. Hold this pose for at least 60 seconds to feel more empowered. This is something extremely freeing as well. There is something about this position that makes you feel invincible and powerful. If you start your day with this boost of energy, it will stay with you all day long.

Whenever you are talking to your boss or someone else you want to impress, then use the wonder woman pose. Start by passing a test, standing with your feet apart, and place your hands on the hips. If your boss joins you in the break room for a cup of coffee, your heartbeat might quicken, and your mind might try to think of an interesting conversation to make. If this is the situation you are in, then channel your inner superwoman by using the wonder woman pose.

If you are nervous about an interview, then use "the performer" poses to increase your confidence. It is quite similar to the salutation pose and is named in honor of Mick Jagger. Opting for a high-power pose while amid an interview can make you seem presumptive, foolish, and even downright offensive. Regardless of how powerful it makes you feel, power poses are not meant for an interview. So, before the interview, find a safe spot yourself and use this pose. You merely need to widen your stance and throw your hands up in the air. It is like the pose a performer on stage would assume to receive applause from an audience. Allow this pose to wash over your body and mind with power and confidence. Hold this pose for a minute or 2 to enable favorable hormonal reactions to take place in your body. Once the time's up, you will feel better than you did before.

Different power positions can be used according to the situation you are in. If you are in the midst of a social event or a social gathering, then another power pose you can use is the Vanna White. Use this power pose whenever you feel a little low in confidence, especially when people surround you. Keep in mind that the basic idea of power positioning is to empower you to access your internal strength, and the simplest way to do this is by taking up a little space. So, you might not be able to outstretch your arms like you did in the salutation position while presenting a business argument, but you can still incorporate certain elements from it to form a new power pose. By stretching your arms and using subtle gestures, you can take up more space than you were doing previously. For instance, if you are in the middle of a presentation, place one hand on the whiteboard or the computer screen or anywhere else, as long as you can outstretch your arm. You can casually rest your other hand on your hips, provided it is a social setting.

Leaning slightly forward onto a desk or the back of a chair is a great power position. Use this position whenever you are presenting any ideas at your workplace or conducting any business deals. Emmy Cuddy named this pose as "the Loomer." She considered this position to be a tribute to the former United States President Lyndon B. Johnson. President Johnson was 6 '4," and he used his physical stature to project confidence and intimidate others.

Whenever you are in a business setting and you feel the need to internalize any negative emotions you are feeling, or want to exhibit power, then use this position. If you are standing, take a second to find a chair or a table nearby and place your hands on the table while leaning forward. Without coming across as overly dominant, this position helps you seem more in control. It places you in control of your audience and shows that you demand respect and power.

Another simple power pose that is subtle but works as well as any other pose is smiling. A confident smile can not only boost your energy and make you feel more comfortable, but it also makes others feel that you are confident. Smiling has the power to influence your mood and the mood of those around you.

The great thing about using power poses is that you can use them whenever you want to. Whenever you want to access your internal stores of confidence and power, opt for a specific pose. You can use power poses before going to a job interview, giving a speech, making a business presentation, having a tough conversation with your significant other, or even before an audition. If you want to do all of this, then there is another option available to you - you can perform power poses as soon as you wake up in the morning. Start your day with a couple of power poses and recharge your body and mind with the power and confidence you want to feel.

Hack #6: Speak Up

A common fear that many people share is the fear of speaking up. The inability to speak up, not just in personal situations, but even in the work environment, can prove detrimental to your growth. If you cannot speak up, then your ability to express yourself will also be hindered. The common doubts like, "What if others don't understand what I'm saying? What if people believe that I am foolish? What will happen if I fumble for words and make a fool of myself?" can silence anyone. This kind of self-doubt can creep up on you and overwhelm you if you aren't careful.

It is easy to hold on to negativity and not say anything. However, if you don't engage in conversation or don't express yourself, you are not solving any problems. No one expects you to speak perfectly or be 100% insightful all the time. It is merely about expressing yourself. Just because you are speaking up and expressing yourself, it doesn't mean you will always contradict others. If you want to become confident, then you need to find your inner voice and be comfortable with expressing yourself. If you are struggling with speaking up, then here are a couple of simple tips you can follow to become more confident.

Start identifying all the situations where you feel comfortable expressing yourself. It could be a personal opinion, emotions, or even feelings. Maybe the situations include ones where you are comfortable with those around you - in the company of your friends, loved ones, family members, or a couple of colleagues. Once you identify a specific situation, ask yourself what is different from that situation and the other one where you struggle to speak. Now think back to how the situation was a year ago. Maybe you were not friends with the people you are friends with right now, and perhaps you were hesitant. So, what changed? When you identify the answer, it becomes easier to start expressing yourself.

If you are afraid of expressing yourself or speaking up in front of a crowd, then take small steps. Maybe you can talk to someone you trust and ask them for their opinion about your ideas. Before you commit to sharing your idea during a meeting, talk to a trusted colleague about them. After this, it becomes easier to share your opinions with no hesitation. If you want to work on improving your confidence levels, then ask for feedback. Ensure that you keep an open mind to whatever feedback you receive. It isn't always going to be positive, and whatever criticism you obtain, take it in your stride and work on improving yourself.

If you want to grow in life, you will need to step outside your comfort zone. To step outside your comfort zone, you will need a little confidence. Work on developing your ability to speak up in a lower risk environment or in a place where you know you have a support system. It could be in the form of a trusted friend, mentor, or even a colleague.

If you do have something important to say and you are hesitating, then write down the things you wish to share. If you are struggling to speak up, you can minimize the chances of stumbling, stuttering, and fumbling for words by making a note of the things you wish to share. It is okay to read out your thoughts, and it doesn't have any negative connotations. If you can express yourself clearly and concisely, then there is no harm in writing down your thoughts and sharing them. Once you write, you get a better perspective of the things you wish to share.

All opinions matter. Regardless of whether they are big or small. You don't have to hold yourself back and wait for the major issues before you start speaking up. You don't have to doubt whether what you are sharing is worth it. Try to understand yourself, but it is important to express yourself. Once you understand the reasons you are supposed to speak up, it becomes easier to share. It also gives you an internal sense of confidence to express yourself clearly and with no hesitation.

Another simple step you can use is to visualize the conversation before it takes place. Maybe you can stand in front of a mirror and practice how you want to speak up. You can concentrate on your body language, the tone of voice you use, and facial expressions while doing this. Before diving in, start visualizing the conversation of the meeting. After you have done this, it becomes easier to articulate your views. This kind of rehearsal comes in handy, and with a little practice, you will see a positive change in the way you can speak up.

If you ever hesitate to voice your opinions, then there are two simple ways in which you can frame your statements. Start by using, "this is why," or "this is what I think." By using these phrases, you will feel more prepared, and confident while expressing yourself. Apart from this, these kinds of comments help further the conversation and attract comments from others.

If you are trying to make a convincing argument or want to get your audience to listen to you, then it is not just about presenting emotions, it is about facts too. Emotions play a big part in this, but facts are equally important. When you share facts or statistics, it makes you sound more confident. Don't allow your emotions to overwhelm you whenever you are speaking out. Regardless of how deeply you feel about a specific topic or an issue, stay rational and don't allow emotions to get the better of you. If you are easily overwhelmed, then take a moment to gather your thoughts, recompose yourself, and then express yourself.

Start using the "act as if" technique discussed in the previous sections to seem more confident. If you want to change yourself, then ensure that you are willing to commit to change yourself consciously. It is not an easy process, but your efforts will pay off eventually. If you are trying to improve your confidence, then try imitating the behavior of someone you admire. If you admire the way your boss always seems confident while expressing himself, then why not try copying his body language? If you admire your parent, friend, colleague, or someone else, then ask yourself what this person would do if he or she was in the same situation that you are in? The answer to this question will give you a plan of action about how you can start speaking up.

A common problem that prevents many people from sharing their beliefs or opinions is that they concentrate too much on the outcome. If you want your voice to be heard, then you need to let go of the sphere. Stop worrying about outcomes to the extent that you forget to live in the moment. If you start sharing and speaking up, it becomes easier to gauge what the outcome will be. Instead of worrying about the outcome, start living in the moment. Regardless of the response you get from others, it is worth speaking out. For instance, if you're worried that you will be criticized for speaking up, then ask yourself what is the worst that others can do? Apart from dealing with criticism, there won't be much else, right? Once you take away the fear of the outcome, it becomes easier to start speaking up.

It is not just your verbal language, but the non-verbal language matters too. Pay attention to your body language, the tone of your voice, the gestures you use, and your facial expressions. These things speak louder than any words you speak. The simplest way to pay attention to all this is by recording yourself. Have an imaginary conversation in front of the camera and look at all the different aspects of your non-verbal communication. Maybe your posture is too dominating, or the tone of voice you use is meek. As and when you notice certain aspects you are supposed to change, start working on improving yourself.

It is not just about speaking up, but you must also be a good listener. Many people talk, but seldom do others listen. If you want to be heard, then they will listen. Notice any behavioral patterns or the style of speaking used by others. It gives you a better idea to understand how or what you're supposed to say. If you think you cannot express yourself in a crowd, then you can seek a one-on-one meeting later. By using your insights from the previous meeting, you can easily get through a personal meeting.

If you notice that someone else is having a tough time to express their opinions, then learn to be an advocate for them. If you notice that someone keeps raising their hand to express an opinion, but gets overlooked, then maybe you can say something like, "I think ___ has something she wants to share." Start speaking up for those who have a tough time expressing yourself. When you help others, it makes you feel more confident.

Once you express yourself, your confidence levels will increase. When you start asserting yourself and hold your ground, it will improve your self-confidence. If you keep doing this at your workplace, you will come across as being an assertive leader.

Hack #7: Love Yourself

Self-esteem and self-confidence are closely related to self-love. Self-love is about taking care of yourself and loving yourself unconditionally. The way you perceive yourself influences the way others perceive you. If you don't feel confident, others will not think of you as a confident woman. Self-confidence stems from self-love. Understand that you deserve to be loved and cherished not just by others, but by yourself. If you don't approve of yourself, you can never be truly confident. You need to understand your self-worth. It is easy to criticize and judge yourself and loving yourself can be difficult. Loving yourself despite all your flaws takes a conscious effort. Once you love yourself, you will see a positive shift in your level of self-confidence. Once you believe in yourself, you can take risks, be spontaneous, and engage in experiences that teach you more about yourself. Take control of your self-confidence by showing yourself the love and compassion you usually show others.

We all tend to have a specific mental picture of ourselves. This self-perception tends to influence your confidence too. Keep in mind that this picture changes based on the different life experiences you have.

If this self-image you have is rather negative, then work on making it more positive. Think about ways in which you can develop yourself to fix this mental self-image.

When you start taking care of your physical appearance, you will feel more confident about yourself. Getting regular haircuts, showering daily, and maintaining general hygiene will make you feel good. For instance, don't you feel good after soaking in the tub for a while after a tiring day? If you do this daily, you will start to feel better.

Pay attention to the clothes you wear. Dress appropriately and dress in a way that enhances your best features. When you dress nicely, you will feel better about yourself, and it will make you feel more confident. Dressing nicely doesn't mean that you must splurge on a new wardrobe. It merely means you need to wear clothes that look good on you. If you want others to take you seriously, then get out of those sweaty pajamas and dress stylishly.

Internal self-talk never really takes a break unless you are asleep. Self-talk is the internal dialogue that keeps going on in your head. This self-talk can be quite damaging when it turns negative. For instance, you might be doing the laundry, then suddenly your mind might tell you it is too difficult and to take a break. Your self-talk can either motivate you or reduce your morale. The great thing is that you are the narrator of this internal dialogue. You can script it any way that you deem fit, and no one can change it. If you think it is taking on a negative hue, fill it with positivity.

If your internal critic keeps telling you that you are not good enough, or that something is too difficult, or that you don't have the skills to get things done, it is time to shut down this kind of self-talk. To do this, you need to pay conscious attention to the thoughts you think. Whenever you notice a negative thought, replace it with a positive one. If you feel like you cannot get something done, then tell yourself you need a while longer than you thought you did. If something seems impossible, tell yourself that it is impossible right now and not forever. You can improve your self-confidence by merely tweaking the way you talk to yourself.

It is not just about thinking positive thoughts, but you need to act on these thoughts as well. Your thoughts will not amount to anything unless you take action. Action is an important step to develop self-confidence. When you start acting on your thoughts, it becomes easier to feel more confident. Instead of telling yourself that you cannot do something, take the first step and challenge your inner beliefs about your abilities and yourself. For instance, if you wish to run a marathon, won't be able to do this overnight. In this case, your mind might tell you that you don't have what it takes to complete a marathon. You can challenge this belief by exercising daily. Within a month, your negative self-talk will reduce.

A common tactic used by great generals in a battlefield is that they thoroughly understand the enemy. If you don't know your enemy, then you cannot defeat him. Are you wondering who your enemy is? Well, you are your worst enemy. You are your worst critic. If you don't keep a check on yourself, you will become critical of everything you do and think. If you are trying to replace a negative self-image with something more positive, then you need to know yourself. Don't ignore your thoughts. Instead, start paying attention to them. Learn to understand why you think the way you think. Once you analyze the reasons, it becomes easier to keep a check on all sorts of negativity. If there are any limitations you have imposed on yourself, then try to see the bigger picture as to why you have these limitations. By understanding yourself inside and out, you can become more confident.

Learn to be kind and generous. Not just toward others, but yourself. If your friend were going through a nasty breakup, how would you deal with her? Would you be compassionate and offer some rational advice? Why don't you extend this compassion toward yourself? Not just others, even you deserve a little compassion. Your self-image will improve when you start being as kind and generous with yourself as you are with others.

The way you speak influences the way others perceive you. Someone in authority always speaks slowly and clearly. It shows confidence. Concentrate on the way you speak to others. If you are always in a rush, it often stems from the belief that whatever you are saying is not worthy of being heard or that you don't have the confidence to express yourself more clearly. Even if you don't feel confident initially, with a little practice, it will come to you naturally. It will make you feel more confident.

If you don't think you'll be able to do something well or excel at something, your confidence takes a beating. To get over this fear, start preparing yourself. You would not go unprepared for a major exam, would you? Likewise, learn to be more prepared for everything that life throws at you. If you are learning a new skill, you might not be confident in your abilities. However, if you practice and keep learning, your confidence levels will improve.

What are your core beliefs or the primary principles upon which you want to lead your life? If you don't want to feel directionless as you wade through the waters of life, you need certain principles. A simple example of a principle would be "to live my life according to my passions," or "I want to learn something new daily." Once you have these basic beliefs in place, it becomes easier to concentrate on any goals you have. All this will make you feel more confident.

Start setting small goals for yourself and work on attaining them. These goals can be related to your personal or professional life. It doesn't matter, as long as you attain your goals. Whenever you feel low on confidence, you will feel better by merely looking at all the goals you have attained. Most of us tend to forget about the small stuff because we concentrate only on the bigger picture. To attain a major life goal, you need to get through various small goals. For instance, if you are trying to lose weight, then a small goal could be to exercise regularly for ten days. Once you attain this goal, it will give you the confidence and motivation required to work towards attaining your big goal.

Another simple aspect of self-love is to learn to be grateful. Learn to be grateful for all the good that you have in your life. Learn to be grateful for every experience you had because it has contributed to your growth. Even if you don't see it immediately, there are plenty of things you have in your life that make you happy. It could be something as simple as having a loving family or a job you enjoy. You probably have things today you did not have a couple of years ago, and you wished for them. Now that you have these things, why don't you be grateful for them? Instead of concentrating on all the things you don't have, concentrate on the good that you do have. When you learn to be grateful for everything you have in your life, for all the things that others have given you, it helps improve your self-image.

We all tend to procrastinate from time to time. Even successful people do this. Take a couple of minutes and think about a specific task or activity you have been procrastinating for a while now. Start making a list of all the things you wish to do but didn't get around to doing them until now. Once you have a list in place, start working on them. As and when you complete an activity, strike it off your list. Whenever you complete something you have been putting off, you will feel better about yourself. It will give you the confidence you require to keep going.

Whenever you have to complete an overwhelming task or project, it can be quite intimidating. It can overwhelm the best of us. Instead of worrying about an overwhelming activity, try breaking it up into smaller, manageable chunks. It becomes easier to complete a task. When a task is perfectly manageable and attainable, completing it is easier. By completing a series of small tasks, you can attain your goal. Apart from this, whenever you complete a small task, it will improve your self-confidence. Your little achievements will soon add up. When you see that you can complete any task, it will boost your motivation too.

Chapter Seven: Confidence in the Workplace

It is difficult to be a woman in a world that's dominated by men. It is even more difficult to be a confident woman in the workplace. Even though we live in the modern world, society still burdens women with ridiculous expectations as if we were still in the dark ages. A common issue that plagues a lot of women is a lack of confidence in the workplace. Most of us worry that we're not good enough or that there is someone who is better than us. If you want to be more confident in your workplace, then here are some tips that you can start following today.

Work with The Team

Try to integrate yourself within the team at work and don't be afraid to speak up. Make an effort to get to know your colleagues, clients, bosses, or anyone else you need to work with. Try to show that you are interested and open to socializing without coming across as being too pushy. Once others know that you are not a tough person to talk to, they will start reaching out to you. It is quintessential that you work on networking with others and create business relationships.

The more you understand about your work environment, the more confident you will feel.

Contribute Strategically

Whenever you work on a specific project, make it a point to actively align your workload and priorities with that of your manager or boss. Think about it from your boss's perspective - what is the most valuable thing that you can do for your boss? It might be tempting to work on projects that are not as important, but it is imperative that you make yourself a valuable asset for your team. When your approach to work is based on the idea to add as much value as you can, the results will also be more valuable, and your work will be more appreciated. If you don't contribute any value, then others will quickly forget about you. Feeling like you are a real member of a team will improve your self-confidence.

Use the Progress Principle

Teresa Amabile, a researcher at Harvard Business School, created the Progress Principle. This principle essentially states that you need to celebrate all the little wins that happened to you in order to have a positive work-life. Once you start tracking your progress and celebrate the progress you make, regardless of whether it is big or small, your productivity will improve. Not just that, but it will also improve your confidence levels. It is easy to keep track of all the work you do. You can use a journal or even an app to keep track of all the tasks you accomplish daily. Once you see the progress you make, your confidence will grow. It is not just about making progress, but you must also learn to appreciate the progress you make. It will make you feel like a valuable asset to your team.

Whenever you feel a little low on confidence, you can go through the progress journal and remind yourself of all that you have accomplished. When you see that you have come a long way from where you started, you will automatically feel better. It tends to create an internal sense of motivation that will fuel your desire to keep growing.

Avoid Comparison

Instead of worrying about what others say and do, concentrate all your energy only on yourself. Nothing can kill your self-confidence as quickly as a comparison does. Keep in mind that every individual is unique, and no two humans are alike. If you keep comparing yourself to others, you are merely wasting your time and energy. These are two precious resources that will not come back once wasted. Everyone is good at something. Instead of worrying about things you are not good at, concentrate on the things that you can excel at. If you feel you lack in a specific area, you can always work on improving your skill set. Keep in mind that it is not the end of the line. The work that you do is meaningful, and you were chosen for your position based on certain qualifications you have. So, never, not even for a second, believe that you are not worthy of the job you do.

Speaking Up

Another thing a lot of women worry about is that others will think they sound stupid. It is a major reason why a lot of people fail, because they believe their ideas aren't worth being expressed or shared. If you think you have a good idea, then speak up and express yourself. If you're hesitant to talk in front of a group, you can always seek a coworker's or trusted friend's opinion about the idea. If you want to be successful at work, make it a habit to share your ideas. Even if others think they are stupid, someone might find your ideas brilliant.

Asking Questions

This point is similar to the previous one. It is not just about sharing your ideas, but don't be afraid to ask questions either. If you don't understand something, ask for an explanation. If you don't know something, then get someone to explain it to you. It doesn't make you stupid to ask questions. Asking questions is the only way in which you can test understanding of a topic. When you understand something, only then will you be able to question your beliefs. Asking questions is a part of the process of learning. Even if others laugh at your questions, don't worry. The joke is on them and not you.

Being Bossy

A lot of women, especially the ones who are higher up the corporate ladder or hold managerial positions, tend to be wary of sharing their opinions. If you are holding yourself back because you're worried you will come across as being bossy by sharing your opinions, then think again. If you don't speak up and keep everything to yourself, others will never know your potential. Apart from this, keep in mind that you are the boss. It is okay to be nice to others. At the same time, you must not forget that you shouldn't be a pushover. Don't allow others to walk all over you. Keep in mind that you have earned your job based on your potential and merit. If your job requires you to supervise others, then do it properly. You don't have to be best friends with everyone you come across in the course of your job. A job is a job, and it is your responsibility to do it well. At times you will need to make certain tough decisions, and it might not sit well with others. All this is part of life. The sooner you make peace with all this, the better you will feel.

Dress Accordingly

The clothes you wear must reflect your confidence. According to your job description, wear clothes that suit your role and responsibility. Don't dress too casually and don't overdress either. Choose conservative clothing whenever it comes to a professional work environment. The clothes you wear must make others take note of you and regard you as a serious professional. Your clothes must convey that you mean business, and nothing else. Avoid wearing flashy and over-the-top outfits. Choose clothes with clean lines and opt for well-tailored jackets and pants. The idea is to opt for such clothes that make you feel comfortable and professional at the same time.

Saying No

Learning to say no is a skill that will come in handy in all aspects of your life. Your ability to say no directly stems from your self-confidence. If you aren't confident, then you will not be able to say no to others. Learning to put your foot down is a great way to ensure that your personal boundaries are not being trespassed. Once you are aware of all the things that are not acceptable to you, it becomes easier to say no. Whenever you are saying no, remember that you're not saying no to the person, but to the task at hand. It means that you are aware of your priorities and understand how to prioritize effectively.

For instance, if a colleague asks you to fill in for him so he can go out and watch a football match, then you don't have to do this. If you think you cannot get on with your work and cover for him, then say no. If you are unable to prioritize your time, then you will never be able to get anything done. Stop being a pushover at work. Once others realize that they can get away with anything without worrying about consequences, they will take you for granted. If you want to be seen as a valuable member of the team, then you need to learn to say no.

Establishing Boundaries

Establish certain boundaries about your work and professional life. If you want to avoid these two aspects of your life from clashing with each other, then you need to establish certain boundaries. For instance, a simple boundary would be to avoid carrying personal baggage to work and avoid working after hours at home. It is quite a simple rule. By doing this, you will feel less burned-out and will have more time to do the things you want. If you have to balance home and work with all the work you do outside, then it is quintessential that you establish boundaries. Regardless of what you do, ensure that you get a little personal time every day. It could be anywhere between 20 minutes to an hour. During this time, concentrate only on yourself. Use this time to do anything that you love. Maybe you can read a book, take a leisurely bath, watch a TV series that you like, or maybe even exercise. Don't forget to concentrate on yourself merely because you must juggle other things in life. If you stop taking care of yourself, it will negatively affect your both personally and professionally.

General Tips

You might be familiar with the saying that you only get one chance to make a first impression, and a first impression lasts a long time. It really is a good reason why you must greet a person by looking them in the eyes and a warm smile on your face. You can project self-confidence by making eye contact and by smiling. Apart from this, your posture, gestures, and the way you carry yourself tells others how confident you are as a person. One of the most effective ways of communicating your sense of confidence to others is through your body language.

Learn to accept all compliments willingly. You don't have to hide your expression of joy from others. Instead of brushing away any compliments, learn to accept them graciously. Giving is an important part of life, but so is receiving. When you receive a compliment willingly and graciously, you show others that you are confident about yourself and are aware of yourself.

Whenever you meet someone for the first time, regardless of having a conversation over the phone or in person, always give your name. When you lead by introducing yourself, it shows you respect yourself and that they should pay attention to whatever you have to say.

Being aware of yourself and your skills is not the same as self-promotion. So, don't brag. Whenever you brag, it shows you are not confident of yourself and are also seeking external approval. A confident person is quite modest. Bragging is also a sign for seeking attention, and the ones who indulge in it use it only because of their low self-worth. Every once in a while, an individual's self-confidence can take a nosedive. If you keep thinking about your difficulties in life or past disappointments, you will only make things worse. The best way to remove any doubt is to increase positive action in your life. Whenever your self-confidence takes a beating, you don't have to overanalyze the situation. Instead, try to do something about it. When you are engaged in work, don't dwell on unnecessary thoughts, and instead focus on coming up with solutions. You might not be able to solve your problem immediately, but the more sense you try to make of it, the easier it will be to tackle the problem.

Whenever you face a challenge or a setback, think of it as an opportunity to learn rather than a failure. When you do this, your general outlook towards life will be more positive. No one is perfect, and everyone has endured failure at some point or another. It does not reflect poorly on your capacity to perform. Therefore, there is no point in allowing it to shatter your confidence. Whenever you feel you are losing perspective, you merely need to regather your thoughts. Take a break from the situation and try to remove yourself physically from the circumstances. By doing this, you will start to feel better.

By following the simple tips discussed in this section, you will become more assertive and confident at work. In fact, most of these steps are applicable to your life in general. During the initial period, you will need to implement these steps consciously. However, after a while, they will come naturally to you. Even if you don't feel confident right now, once you practice these tips, you will feel confident. You cannot become confident overnight. But with a little practice, patience, consistency, and self-care, you can improve your confidence levels.

Chapter Eight: Dating Confidence Hacks

Confidence is perhaps the most desirable and irresistible trait when it comes to dating. It's not just about looking attractive in dating, but it is about having self-confidence. When you are self-confident, it shows others that you know what you want and is not afraid to get it. Everyone wants to date someone who has confidence and has a strong sense of self-worth. A confident person looks approachable, is happy, and walks with a sense of determination. Nothing can replace confidence and learning to be confident is quintessential in every aspect of your life. The great thing about confidence is that it is not based on luck, anyone can develop self-confidence.

A confident person never feels like they are missing out on anything in life. They don't get caught up worrying about the things that can go wrong or possible rejection. Instead, they concentrate on all the good that they have and the possibility of something good coming their way. They don't feel threatened easily and stay calm even in testing circumstances. In stark contrast to this, a person running low on self-confidence gets scared easily and feels anxious or threatened whenever something doesn't go their way. They worry too much about the things that can go wrong in this process; they forget to think about all the things that are going well for them.

When it comes to dating, a confident person would think, "If I don't ask him out, I will not have a date. If I do ask him out, I at least stand a chance." In contrast to this, a person with low levels of confidence takes dating quite personally. If things don't work out like they hoped they would, they blame themselves.

Clarity About Self-Worth

You don't worry about how others perceive you. Since you already know that you are good, the way you are and are lovable, you believe that the other person will also see the same. A confident woman would not worry whether or not other men like her. If you want to be confident, then try to understand that your self-worth comes from within. Your self-worth must be independent of what the guy thinks of yours. You don't have to worry about his feelings and certainly don't have to feel stressed if his feelings are unclear. Instead, you will start working on the assumption that you are worthy of being loved unconditionally.

Set and Implement Boundaries

Self-esteem and personal boundaries are interrelated. When you know your needs and wants, it becomes easier to establish certain boundaries to determine what is and isn't acceptable to you. When you are aware of these boundaries, it becomes easier to steer clear of any pressure to do something you don't want. You cannot set or implement boundaries when you don't care and respect yourself. You are the only person who has the power to determine what your needs are. You don't have to do things because it would make your potential partner happy. You don't have to change yourself to find true love.

When you don't have any boundaries or have weak boundaries, then you might start compromising too much and will eventually lose the ability to see things objectively

When you are uncertain about your wants and needs, you cannot expect your partner to know what you want. You need to be clear about yourself, your expectations, and your needs. Only then will you be able to give yourself fully to a relationship. By establishing and implementing certain personal boundaries, you can ensure that you stay true to yourself. Losing your authentic self for the sake of a relationship is never a healthy sign. The best way to avoid your self-esteem and self-confidence from taking a beating is by establishing personal boundaries.

Avoid Over Personalization

If something goes wrong, keep in mind that you are not the only one involved in the relationship. The success or failure of a relationship is based on the partners involved. Neither partner can take all the credit when things go right, and neither should take the blame if everything is flawed. A confident woman understands that it is not fully her fault if a relationship fails. With the right attitude, you will be able to dissect the relationship and understand any mistakes you make carefully. Even if you don't click with someone, rest easy knowing that there is something else in store for you. If you don't find your match immediately, it doesn't mean the end of the road. It merely means you need to look further.

When you're no longer insecure about yourself and your needs, it becomes easier to find a potential partner. Stop obsessing and overanalyzing every interaction that took place in an attempt to uncover what you did wrong. A relationship is a two-way street, and you should not be too hard on yourself.

Don't Have to Show Off

Keep in mind that a woman who is confident about her capabilities will not try to show off or talk herself up. You will not feel like doing these things because you are secure about who you are as a person. Only those who are insecure or feel they are unworthy are the ones who try to hide their insecurity by constantly bragging. If you want to seem like a confident woman while dating, avoid bragging about yourself. If your date brags about himself and keeps talking himself up, then it is a sign that he is rather insecure.

Confidence doesn't come from having to praise oneself constantly. Instead, it is an internal sense of satisfaction that makes you feel good without having to talk about it. When you feel you are worthy of something, you don't have to talk to people about it. It shows in the way you think, believe, and act. Keep in mind that you don't have to sell yourself. Whenever you are out on a date, it is not a sales pitch, and all that you need to do is to be your genuine self.

Trust Your Decisions

A key to having high self-confidence is believing in yourself and trusting your ability to choose wisely. Apart from this, when you are confident you will be equipped to deal with any situation, even if it doesn't play out like you thought it would. Even when things go awry, it will come with self-confidence. Don't constantly second-guess their actions or feel conflicted about doing or saying the right thing. When you are true to your authentic self and are comfortable in your skin, then you will be able to express how you feel precisely.

On the other hand, a woman with low self-esteem will often question her judgment, will not trust gut instincts, and will be afraid of doing or saying something wrong. Because of all these fears, anxiety and self-doubt become her natural way of life. If this is how you feel, don't be afraid to keep developing your self-confidence.

Accepting Responsibility

A true sign of confidence is accepting responsibility for one's emotions and feelings. Keep in mind that you are only responsible for the way you think and feel. You are not responsible for the way your partner feels. If something makes them feel a specific way, then it is not your problem. If your date blames you for something you didn't do, you don't have to take responsibility. Relationships are about compromise, but you don't have to be the only one who keeps compromising all the time. You need to take responsibility for your acts, both good and bad. If you make any mistakes, think of them as learning opportunities to make yourself better in the future. If something didn't work, then it is not entirely your fault.

The Way It Is

A confident woman feels secure in her relationship. If you don't feel secure about yourself, your partner, or even the relationship, then what's the point? You don't necessarily need a title of some sort to confirm the relationship. If you can sustain yourself in the relationship with no external force or pressure, then it is a healthy relationship.

If your relationship is a certain way, then that's how things are. Don't expect it to be something else, or don't lull yourself into thinking that it is something else. Don't try to change yourself or your partner for the sake of the relationship. If things are meant to last, then they will. If it wasn't meant to be, then it is a learning lesson for you.

Holding On

If it looks like things are not working out, or that you are stuck in a toxic relationship, then have the strength to move on. A confident woman knows that it is not in her best interest to stay in a bad or a toxic relationship. If you value yourself and respect yourself, then you will want to be appreciated for who you are. If you don't love yourself, you cannot expect anyone else to love you. If you have a negative relationship with your inner self, then you will just keep attracting negative people in your life. Understand that people can cause damage only if you let them. If you feel like you're being treated unfairly or that the treatment doled out to you as an acceptable, then move on. Nothing is worth sacrificing your self-esteem.

Don't Need Any Reassurance

All those who have self-confidence and self-esteem know that they are lovable and are loved. They certainly don't need a guide to remind them of their self-worth. When you are insecure, you tend to constantly seek validation from external sources, and become resentful when you don't get it. You might even end up blaming your partner by saying that he makes you feel insecure or unworthy of being loved. The harder you try to please the other person, the more damage it does to your self-worth. An insecure person always seems needy, and no one likes a needy person. If you don't feel good about yourself, then there is nothing in this world that can ever make you feel better. Even if you feel good when you are reassured, it is only temporary. This feeling needs to come from within. Unless it comes from within, your life will not go anywhere that you want it to.

When it comes to finding your partner, ensure that your heart does not solely guide your decision. At times, the heart is blinded to what the mind sees. Trust your instinct, consider your rational part of the mind, and follow your heart. Once you are guided to all these three things, you are bound to make the right decision. Don't second-guess yourself. Even if there is a moment of self-doubt, try to understand why this self-doubt stems from it. Don't try to repress or suppress any emotions or feelings. Instead, work on analyzing them and understanding them. Everything that you feel defines you as a person.

Chapter Nine: Taking Care of Yourself

When you take care of yourself and your health, your overall approach toward life improves. Self-care, or caring face else, is amongst the primary ways in which you can control your overall wellbeing. When you don't take care of yourself, your overall wellness suffers in numerous ways. Your overall wellbeing is a combination of various lifestyle factors that work together to bring about a sense of overall peace, happiness, and health. Self-esteem is your ability to believe in yourself, your skills, and your ability to get things done. To assess your self-esteem, you need to concentrate on your self-worth. Your self-worth is influenced to a great extent by the degree of your health and wellness. If you are healthy, then your self-worth increases and benefits the way you perceive yourself. It also affects your wellness. If your overall outlook of yourself is rather negative, then your wellness suffers.

On the other hand, self-care is a simple term that defines the way you treat yourself. Self-esteem is more about taking care of your mental and emotional wellbeing, whereas self-care is about taking care of your physical, financial, and mental wellbeing. It could be something as small as getting a massage after a long day, or going to bed early and getting the type of rest that your body requires. Your self-care routine is what you make of it, and it is the basis for your overall health and wellbeing.

If you're not good at loving yourself, you will find it incredibly difficult to love anyone else. Apart from this, you will also find it difficult to accept love. Self-care is an ongoing journey, and it includes a variety of things. It is something you need to do daily if you want to improve the quality of your life. If you want to feel happy, self-assured, and balanced in life, then self-care must be your priority. Unless you make yourself a priority, you cannot start living the life you want. Therefore, it is safe to say that your self-esteem, self-confidence, and self-care are all associated. If you take care of yourself, you will notice a positive change in your self-confidence.

Tech Detox

We all live in a world that's dominated by technology. In fact, technology surrounds us all the time. From the moment we wake up until the moment we sleep at night, we spend a lot of time on our mobile phones, laptops, television screens, and plenty of other gadgets. Ensure that you enjoy at least an hour of tech-free time daily. Keep your phone away, forget about all the emails, and concentrate only on yourself. All these things can be attended to later, you don't have to worry about it right now. This is also a great way in which you can forget about the worries of your usual routine.

Concentrate on Your Diet

When your body gets all the nutrition it requires, the way it functions improves. If you want to improve your overall health and wellbeing, then you need to have a sound nutritional plan in place. Ensure that your daily diet consists of plenty of fresh fruits, vegetables, lean protein, dietary fiber, and at least eight glasses of water. Most of us are often in a hurry to get through our day, and we tend to eat our meals on the go. Instead, pay attention to what, when, and how much you eat. Make a conscious habit of sitting down while eating. Learn to be grateful for every meal you eat and practice mindful eating. Pay attention to the different flavors in the food you eat and thoroughly enjoy every morsel. Once you start taking care of the food you use to fuel your body, you will see a change in your physical health.

Me Time

Regardless of how hectic your daily life gets, ensure that you set certain time aside for yourself. Schedule at least an hour of "me time" into your daily routine. This is one of the simplest ways in which you can incorporate self-care into your daily regime. If one hour seems too much to you, then maybe you can settle for 15 to 20 minutes. During this period, don't concentrate on anything else except yourself. Use this time to read a book, catch up on some sleep, or maybe even write in a journal. Do whatever you want that makes you happy during this period. You can also use this for self-reflection. Simply turn off your mind and allow yourself to feel, think, and believe whatever you want.

Mindfulness

Mindfulness is steadily gaining popularity as a great means of improving one's overall wellbeing. Mindfulness is frequently used in meditation, as it merely means that you are supposed to concentrate all your mental energy on being present. If you want to deal with stress and reduce any anxiety you experience, then start practicing mindfulness. Most of us tend to spend a lot of time thinking about the past or worrying about the future. Well, your past cannot be changed, and the future cannot be fully controlled. So, what is the point in wasting your time thinking about all this? Instead, learn to concentrate on the present. Learn to live in the moment and experience your life right now. By living in the moment, you can improve your mind's ability to focus and concentrate on your goals at hand. This practice can help improve your physical and mental wellbeing.

Exercise

You need to engage in some form of physical activity. Exercise and proper nutrition are key to maintaining good health. Try to exercise as frequently as possible. If you cannot exercise daily, then maybe you can exercise thrice every week. You don't necessarily have to go to the gym to exercise. In fact, there are various fun activities that you can indulge in to exercise all the muscles in your body. Find an activity that you enjoy and start practicing it daily. It could be something as simple as going for a jog, running, biking, hiking, or even swimming. As long as you enjoy the activity, it will not feel like a chore to you. In fact, it could be a great stress buster as well. Whenever you engage in physical activity, your body produces endorphins. Endorphins are feel-good chemicals that help tackle the stress you experience.

Stop Overthinking

Once the simplest sources of stress and anxiety are overthinking. We often get stuck up on the idea that everything needs to be perfect, or else it is not good enough. Give yourself a break and stop chasing the elusive idea of perfection. Perfection is an abstract concept at best, and it doesn't exist in reality. You can try to be the best version of yourself, but it doesn't have to be perfect. Overthinking not only worsens your levels of anxiety, but it can even easily overwhelm you. For instance, when it comes to dieting, if you overthink about what to eat when to eat and how much to eat, it can lead to unnecessary anxiety. This is one of the reasons that it is better to concentrate on your goals and just complete all the tasks it takes to meet the specifics of your goal. At times, the simplest solution is just to get started. Once you take the first step, it becomes easier. When you get into the flow of doing things, the obstacles that seemed overwhelming a while ago will not seem that scary.

Professional Growth

When you start concentrating on your professional growth, you will feel good about yourself. Start setting small goals for yourself at your work and put in the effort required to attain these goals. By doing this, it becomes easier to accomplish your major goals. Whenever a goal overwhelms you, divide it into smaller and more attainable goals. By attaining these smaller goals, you will get the motivation and encouragement required to work toward attaining the major goals.

Inner Child

What were the different activities that you used to enjoy as a child? Don't allow your inner child to grow old. Instead, make it a point to reconnect with your inner child. Maybe you loved riding a bike when you were a kid. So, why don't you ride a bike now? You might even feel like a kid again. This is a great way in which you can forget about all the worries of your adult life and return to your happy childhood. Reconnecting with your inner child, you will feel recharged, revitalized, and happier than before.

Fresh Air

Make a point to spend at least 15 to 20 minutes outdoors daily. Get some fresh air and get away from the four walls of your concrete residence. Most of us are confined to our desktops and then to the four walls of our houses. Avoid doing this. Your body needs a little fresh air. It could be something as simple as going on a walk after dinner. Stop for a moment, smell the roses, appreciate the nature around you and be grateful.

Being Grateful

Take a few minutes and think about all those bits of your life that you are grateful for. It could be something big or small. Things that you are proud of, the things that make you smile, the things you enjoy, the people who mean a lot to you, and those whom you are grateful to have around yourself. You can do this anywhere you are. You can do this while at work, while working out, or even while traveling. When you start feeling sheer gratitude, it is not possible to feel any form of negative emotions like stress or anger. We all must have things that make us instantly happy. The things that make you smile, inspire you, or simply make you happy. It could be a movie, a song, a video, a specific book, or even a friend. Make sure you keep track of these things. Spend a few minutes and make this list. Keep adding on things whenever you notice that something puts a smile on your face. The next time you are feeling low, just refer to this list.

Loved Ones

The company you surround yourself has a positive effect on your overall wellbeing. When you are surrounded by people who love and support you, you will automatically feel better. Start eliminating toxic people out of your life. You don't need any form of toxicity in your life. Whenever you notice that certain people don't contribute to your growth or keep discouraging you from growing, then cut ties with such people. Even if you think you love them, if they don't add some value to your life, you don't need them. When you are surrounded by people who are ambitious, happy, and confident and wish the best for you, your spirits will lift too. So, start paying attention to the company you keep.

When you are feeling low, the last thing you would want to do is to be around other people. Resist doing this at any cost. Life is about forming relationships and connections. The ones you love can change your mood in an instant. Make sure you choose people carefully. You need people who are positive and who will bring positivity into your life. Anyone who wouldn't fit this bill is certainly not worth your while. Stay away from negative people and all forms of negativity.

Being selfless can make you happy too. Do something good for someone else. This is bound to make you feel better about yourself.

It could be something as simple as just holding the door open for someone or letting someone else ahead of you in a queue. It doesn't have to be anything extravagant. The smallest of deeds can make you feel happy.

By following the tips given in this section, you can make self-care a part of your daily routine. By concentrating on your self-care, you can improve your overall sense of wellbeing and confidence. If you want to be a confident adult, then you must not ignore the importance of self-care.

Chapter Ten: Influential Women on Confidence

Having confidence is a lifelong journey full of difficulties. All famous and successful people often seem to give out vibes of self-assurance from every fiber of their being. For most people, becoming self-confident has been a process of ongoing evolution. In this chapter, let us look at famous women who managed to overcome their insecurities and increase their levels of self-confidence.

Serena Williams

In an interview, Serena Williams once said that people probably couldn't relate to her because she is strong, powerful, confident, and black. She was often criticized because her arms were not like the other girls', her legs might not look like someone else's, and her body didn't fit the societal notions of an ideal woman's body. She had plenty of criticism to deal with before she became one of the best tennis players the world has ever seen. So how did she deal with all these haters? Well, the solution was simple. She believed that if someone didn't like her, she didn't have to like them. She believes that loving yourself regardless of what others think about you is the only way we can deal with all the negativity. By not spending all her energy worrying about fitting the notions that others had in their heads, she could excel in her career.

The takeaway from Serena Williams's life lesson is to stop worrying about what society thinks and instead concentrate on improving yourself.

Michelle Obama

Michelle Obama believes that she found her voice when she was young. She isn't aware of when it happened, but she remembers the different experiences that led to it. She counts herself to be amongst the most fortunate women who discovered the voice early because she had an older brother, and she had an incredibly close relationship with her parents. She was always involved in different discussions at the dinner table and was never treated differently from her brother. So, if her father taught her brother to play a specific sport, he taught Michelle the sport too. She had a certain degree of reinforcement from the men in her life which made her confident. Apart from that, her mother always encouraged her to express her ideas freely. Michelle's parents never spoke to her like she was a kid, they instead treated her like a mini adult.

The takeaway from Michelle Obama's life lesson is to freely express oneself without having any qualms about what others will think.

Janelle Monae

The world knows Janelle Monae as a popular artist and a famous singer. In an interview, she confessed that she wasn't always as confident as she is today. She also said that she has moments when she doesn't feel confident now and then. She got tired of feeling like this. She realized that, at the end of the day, she's the only one who has to deal with herself. She grew up in a family of strong women and matriarchs who stepped up and provided for the family even when there were no men around. Being around strong and confident women inspired her to be more confident in herself.

The takeaway from Janelle Monae's life lesson is to accept the simple fact that you are the only one who can influence the way you think.

Mindy Kaling

In an interview, Mindy Kaling said that when she gets asked the same question again and again for years on end, all the words of her answer tend to lose their meaning, even for herself. While talking about confidence, people often talk about supportive parents or a strong sense of self. Apart from these obvious things, different situations shape a person. She wasn't always as confident as she seems today. Like everyone else, she too had moments of extreme self-doubt where she felt stupid, unattractive, and unskilled. When she started working on the set of The Office, she didn't have much self-confidence. Whenever Greg Daniels used to enter the room to talk to the team, she used to raise and lower her chair as a nervous tick. She stayed anxious and kept up with the habit until one of the writers of the show asked her to stop. This just shows that confidence isn't something that a select few are blessed with. It is an ongoing journey.

The takeaway from Mindy Kaling's life journey is that anyone can become confident, provided one decides to make the conscious effort required to learn and develop this skill.

Conclusion

By now you should have a clear idea of what confidence is all about, and different ways in which you can develop self-confidence. By developing your self-confidence, you can start living the life you have always wanted and become more assertive, happy, and stress-free.

Now all that's left for you to do is start implementing all the different practical tips given in this book. Initially, you will be required to make some conscious effort and work on developing these habits. Whenever you notice any negativity creeping up or notice that you are falling back into your old patterns, take a break and work on yourself. Keep in mind that you are the creator of your own beliefs and understand that you have the ultimate power to change the way you feel about yourself and the specific situation. There is more to life, provided you make an effort to change yourself. You don't have to allow any negative self-beliefs to hold you back.

Once you follow the different tips given in this book, you will see a positive change in your life within no time. A little bit of effort, a conscious commitment, and patience are all that you need to stay on the right track.

Resources

https://weheartit.com/articles/328434240-you-re-a-goddess-the-modern-mentality-on-self-esteem

https://www.youtube.com/watch?v=ivNNgdCsY7o

https://www.sciencetimes.com/articles/17703/20170801/wearing-makeup-gives-women-confidence-and-makes-them-feel-smarter.htm,

https://www.nytimes.com/roomfordebate/2013/01/02/does-makeup-hurt-self-esteem/look-your-best-feel-your-best

https://www.wikihow.com/Be-Confident-in-Your-Looks, https://blog.michaelajedinak.com/2017/09/how-to-look-good-and-feel-confident/

https://www.gabrielacruz.ca/6-steps-to-a-goddess-mindset/

https://www.psychologytoday.com/us/blog/changepower/201605/the-9-superpowers-your-smile

https://www.briantracy.com/blog/general/how-a-smile-can-affect-self-esteem-building-healthy-relationships-with-a-positive-attitude/

https://www.anewmode.com/dating-relationships/confident-people-differently-dating-relationships/4/

https://liveboldandbloom.com/10/self-confidence/lack-of-confidence

www.ingramcontent.com/pod-product-compliance
Lightning Source LLC
Chambersburg PA
CBHW070048230426
43661CB00005B/820